# Guidelines for
# Application Integration

patterns & practices

ISBN: 0-7356-1848-8

# Contents

# 1

# Introduction

Welcome to *Guidelines for Application Integration*. Most organizations today use an increasing number of applications and services to solve specific business problems. In many cases, these applications and services exist on different platforms and were created at different times. The challenge that most organizations now face is to provide a method by which these applications can work together to address business goals that constantly evolve.

This guide examines in detail what application integration means and describes the capabilities needed to enable application integration. It discusses the major challenges involved and shows how you can adapt your application integration environment to meet those challenges. It also examines the Microsoft® software products and services you can use to help you design your application integration environment.

After reading this guide, you should be able to determine the requirements for application integration in your organization. The guide is not designed to show exactly which technologies to use in your integration solution. Instead, it focuses on the concepts that apply, regardless of the technologies you currently deploy in your environment.

## Who Should Read This Guide

This guide is written for technical decision makers and architects of organizations that are trying to determine whether they require application integration capabilities, that have already determined that they require application integration, or that want to improve their current application integration environment.

The guide does not provide a detailed analysis of how Microsoft products and services provide application integration; rather it discusses the issues at a more abstract and architectural level that applies to the products and services provided by any company. This guide does discuss, generally, how Microsoft can help you provide an application integration solution, but for more detail, you should examine the information available with each product.

Organizations of almost any scale may require application integration. Although application integration problems are usually more urgent in larger organizations, this guide makes no specific assumptions about the size of organization involved, or about the particular types of applications and services involved.

## Prerequisites

This guide does not require knowledge about any particular programming languages or products. To gain the most benefit from this guide, however, you should understand the issues and problems associated with designing and maintaining applications in an enterprise environment.

# How This Guide Is Organized

This guide is organized into chapters and an appendix as follows.

### Chapter 1: Introduction

The remainder of this chapter introduces important application integration concepts. It discusses the business and technical problems that an application integration solution can mitigate, and examines some implementation choices for your application integration environment.

### Chapter 2: Defining Your Application Integration Environment

To build an effective application integration environment, you need to understand the business problems you need to solve, and what you need from your application integration environment to solve them. This chapter outlines some of the important challenges and illustrates how your application integration environment can meet those challenges.

### Chapter 3: Security and Operational Considerations

An effective application integration solution provides functionality that will rapidly become invaluable to your organization, so it is vital that you carefully design your application integration solution. This chapter discusses the security and operations considerations you need to examine to ensure that your application integration environment continues to operate in a reliable and secure fashion.

### Chapter 4: Using Microsoft Technologies for Application Integration

Microsoft offers a number of products and services that can help you create your application integration environment. This chapter discusses the capabilities of these products and shows how you can use them in your application integration environment.

### Appendix: Application Integration Capabilities

The appendix examines in more detail the application integration capabilities discussed throughout this guide. Use the appendix as reference to clarify how the guide defines these capabilities.

# What Is Application Integration?

Your organization probably uses many applications and services that were built over many months or years, as new business needs were identified. As a result, these applications probably are of different ages, were written by different people using different languages and technologies, reside on different hardware platforms, use different operating systems, and provide very different functionality. In fact, many of your applications often have very little in common at all, resulting in isolated functionality and multiple instances of the same data. For your organization, these conditions can result in redundant activities, higher costs, and inefficient response to your customers.

If you have read this far, your organization has probably identified a business requirement for applications to work together. Just as employees have to work together to meet business goals, your applications need to do the same.

This guide defines application integration as follows:

*Application integration is the secure and orchestrated sharing of processes and/or data between applications within the enterprise.*

Although this definition restricts integration to sharing within the boundaries of an enterprise, the guidelines described in this document also help in providing integration between different enterprises.

Effective application integration can provide your organization with the following important business benefits:

- Allowing applications to be introduced into the organization more efficiently and at a lower cost
- Allowing you to modify business processes as required by the organization
- Providing more delivery channels for your organization
- Allowing you to add automated steps into business processes that previously required manual intervention

## Types of Application Integration

Application integration can be broadly categorized into three types:

- Manual application integration
- Semi-automated application integration
- Fully automated application integration

Most environments involve a combination of all three types. The following paragraphs describe each type in more detail.

### Manual Application Integration

Manual application integration requires people (employees and customers) to act as the interfaces between applications and enable the integration between them. This form of application integration is very common. As an example, think of a customer service department that takes information from the public. People may enter the same information into multiple systems and read information from those systems to respond to customer requests. In other cases, a person may need to read customer information from one database, and then reenter it into another database used for another purpose.

This form of integration requires very little technology investment. It becomes more complex, however, when your organization becomes more complex, and can lead to inaccuracies in data. As the amount and complexity of your data increases, or as the number of applications increases, you will require more and more people to maintain such an environment. An environment that relies heavily on manual integration is generally very inefficient, and does not grow as easily as environments that use more automated techniques.

### Semi-Automated Application Integration

Semi-automated application integration combines human steps with some automation. The person may be involved in an area where the corresponding automated solution is too difficult or expensive to implement, or where the business requires a person to make decisions. For example, your business may require a manager to approve all expense claims. In this case, all of the steps before and after managerial approval may be automated, but a person is required in the middle of the process. In other cases, human intervention may be needed to transform data that is required in another system.

Semi-automated application integration generally requires more technology investment, but once that investment is made, you can often reduce the number of people involved in integrating your applications. Reducing human involvement in this manner usually reduces costs and increases reliability.

### Fully Automated Application Integration

Fully automated application integration removes people from the business process entirely, although they are required to maintain the solution. This type of integration consists of applications communicating through a series of interfaces and adapters. For example, two databases might share data, which is automatically transformed and committed to the second database from the first with no human interaction.

Although fully automated application integration removes the dependency on people, such systems can be more expensive to implement and may not be practical for many business problems. In many cases, you will still require people to make business decisions, and often it is more efficient to have a person control a technical process as well. For these reasons, you should decide where fully automated application integration is appropriate on a case-by-case basis.

## Choosing the Right Types of Application Integration

Each type of application integration has its own set of costs and benefits, as outlined in Table 1.1.

**Table 1.1: Costs and Benefits of Application Integration**

| Application integration type | Costs | Benefits |
| --- | --- | --- |
| Manual | Higher labor costs that scale badly. Subject to human error. | Little change required from existing low-technology environment. |
| Semi-automated | Higher technology costs to implement. Subject to design-time and run-time errors. | Lower labor costs. Scales better. Less subject to human error at run time. Faster processing. |
| Fully automated | Highest technology costs to implement. Subject to design errors. | Lowest labor costs. Not subject to human error at run time. Lose human decision making on business processes, but faster processing. |

Almost all environments involve a combination of all three types of application integration. Of course, in many cases people add to the effectiveness in your business processes. Situations where people often prove essential to effective business processes include:

- **Business process exception handling**. Many different events can lead to a business process exception. They can result from human error at some point in a process, faulty logic (in the applications or in application integration), concurrency issues, or errors in data received from business partners. Because it is not possible to estimate all the possible errors and their corresponding fixes, it is not possible to totally automate responses to business process exceptions.

You need the ability to manually intervene in the business process in some cases and make the appropriate correction without being restricted by what the system is expecting.

- **Manual override of business rules**. Your applications will use business rules that are specific to the context of the enterprise at run time. These business rules facilitate automated execution of your business processes. However, you will need people to intervene in these business rules occasionally—for example, when shipping costs are waived for a large order from a regular customer. A fully automated solution with no manual override cannot allow for exceptions to be made based on human interaction with customers.

- **Approvals at key points within a workflow**. Workflows in your organization can often be automated as long as the values of selected parameters fall within predefined limits. Transactions with values exceeding these limits usually require human approval to make sure that they are reasonable. For example, even if the processing and approval of expense reports within a specified amount is automated, you should ensure that validation by appropriate management personnel occurs if the amount exceeds a predefined limit.

- **System breakdown**. A fully automated solution is completely dependent on the proper functioning of every component application that is part of the overall solution. Manual intervention enables you to temporarily replace a broken link in the chain of integrated applications with human transfer of information. For example, you may need to manually enter orders in applications that are ordinarily received by Electronic Data Interchange (EDI) if the EDI network you access is temporarily down due to a power outage.

If you closely examine processes that involve people, you can identify areas where semi-automated and fully automated business processes can be used. By doing so, you can reduce the number of employees involved in application integration and increase your potential for cost savings and scalability in your organization.

## Making Application Integration Scalable

An important part of making application integration scalable is to increase the number of automated steps and reduce the number of human steps. This generally involves creating interfaces between applications along with predefined logic that replaces human involvement.

Increasing the level of automation generally increases the amount of information traveling between applications without increasing the number of employees required to support the environment. The scalability issues, however, do not stop at simple automation. You should also consider the number of applications themselves and how integration occurs between them. For automated application integration, you have two choices:

- Point-to-point model
- Integration hub model

The following paragraphs discuss each of these in turn.

### Point-to-Point Model

The point-to-point model describes a decentralized structure in which each application communicates directly with the other applications. This type of integration is most appropriate for organizations that need to integrate a few applications with a small number of services.

Figure 1.1 shows the number of connections required for point-to-point environments with three and 10 applications, respectively, when you need to ensure that all applications can communicate with each other.

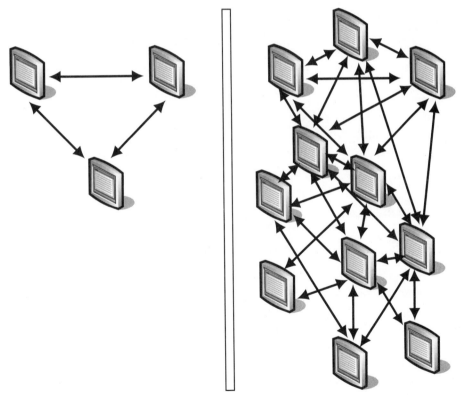

**Figure 1.1**
*Point-to-point communication among applications*

As the number of applications and services increases, the number of interfaces and connections that need to be maintained in a point-to-point environment rapidly increases.

The maximum number of connections required is defined as follows:

$$\sum x \ (x=1 \text{ to } n\text{-}1)$$

where $n$ is the number of applications you need to integrate. The number of interfaces may be up to twice the number of connections (depending on whether they are one-way or two-way interfaces).

This means that for the three application example (Scenario A in Figure 1.1), up to three connections and up to six interfaces are needed, whereas for the 10 application example (Scenario B), up to 45 connections and up to 90 interfaces are required.

In a point-to-point integration environment, interfaces between the applications are usually written as business needs arise. The problem with this approach is the lack of consistency. The integration approach used generally depends on which integration approach the developer is most familiar with, what he or she knows about the individual applications, and so on. As more and more applications are developed or updated, additional interfaces must be created.

The same problem pertains when new business goals are defined that require applications to communicate with one another differently. Every change makes the environment more difficult to understand, until eventually the structure is so complex that it is almost impossible to manage effectively. Such a complex structure may even hinder the company's ability to strategically shift its business goals, due to the high IT costs surrounding the change. Defining application integration on the fly in this way can massively increase your medium-term and long-term costs for a short-term gain.

## Integration Hub Model

The integration hub model provides a more centralized structure, in which an integration hub is placed between the applications, and each application communicates with the hub rather than communicating directly with other applications.

Each application needs only an interface and a connection to the integration hub. To simplify matters, the integration hub can rely heavily on existing standards, which means that either the interfaces already exist or the methodologies for writing them are well-defined.

The main advantage of an integration hub environment is scalability. Figure 1.2 shows the use of an integration hub, again in environments with three and 10 applications, respectively.

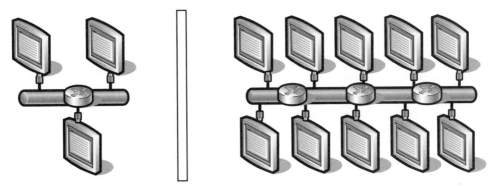

**Figure 1.2**
*Applications connected through an integration hub*

In Figure 1.2, a single connection is required to the integration hub, with interfaces potentially required at the application and the integration hub. However, many environments require only one interface (or none if the application already uses the standards supported by the hub). This configuration leads to a maximum of three connections and six interfaces for the three application example, or 10 connections with 20 interfaces for the 10 application example. In most cases, the number of interfaces will be significantly lower.

The integration hub model is significantly more scalable for integration environments with many applications. A typical large-scale organization has thousands of islands of information, involving thousands of applications. You simply cannot create individual interfaces for every point of interaction. Instead, the solution is to create an application integration environment that allows all of your applications to communicate in a logical, predefined way. This hub infrastructure enables you to modify or update elements much more easily, and to do so when the business requires, rather than when the preexisting technology dictates. It should also allow the organization to more easily change direction and to use the products and services it has to match evolving requirements.

Because interfaces are within the integration hub (and are usually standards-based), you do not need to rewrite them whenever new applications are introduced. However, the hub can be technically challenging to implement and may be too costly for more simple application integration environments. In addition, you may have to sacrifice some data complexity to ensure that each application conforms to the standards of the integration hub.

### Choosing an Application Integration Model

As you examine the specifics of your environment, you will need to determine whether a point-to-point model, an integration hub model, or a combination of the two is most appropriate. Realistically, the decision you make will based on cost and value. In many cases, application integration involves a combination of both models, using point-to-point initially, and then moving to the use of one or more integration hubs as complexity increases and when there are clear business benefits to doing so.

# Requirements for Application Integration

Application integration isn't easy, hence the need for this guide. Typically, an environment that supports application integration meets at least the following requirements:

- Connectivity between different platforms
- Processing of complex business rules, including complex data transformation logic
- Support for business processes, from the very short to the very long, including processes that last weeks or months as data is passed and processed through different parts of the organization
- The ability to modify existing business processes or create new ones as business goals change
- The ability to adapt to changes in hardware, software, and business goals

To help meet these requirements, your application integration environment should:

- Expose a common interface through which applications can communicate, by using business semantics to request Web services.
- Allow service requests at the functional or data level for applications that do not support using business semantics.
- Use a common set of process and service rules to ensure consistency and reuse of integration services.
- Be capable of reusing the existing transport protocols that already exist in the enterprise.
- Insulate itself from existing technologies by using interfaces.

An application integration environment should not depend on the implementation of any particular technology. You don't know what applications and hardware your organization will be using in five years, but whatever they are, your organization will need to support them.

# Implementing Application Integration

You can implement application integration in a wide variety of ways. Common choices include:

- Web services
- Extract, Transform, and Load (ETL)
- Communications message protocols
- Screen scraping
- Program calls
- Direct data access
- File transfer
- Human involvement

The following paragraphs discuss each of these choices in turn.

## Web Services

A Web service is an application component that:

- Exposes useful functionality to other Web services and applications through standard Web service protocols.
- Provides a way to describe its interfaces in detail, allowing developers to build client applications that talk to it. The description is provided in an XML document called a Web Services Description Language (WSDL) document.
- Describes its messages by using an XML schema.

Many vendors have endorsed and have started to provide Web service capabilities in their platforms. Using Web services for integration ensures that your integration is based on open standards that are language neutral and platform independent, and helps to ensure that the technology remains relevant over time.

Web services rely on defined specifications to allow systems from various vendors to interoperate. Web services specifications, commonly referred to as WS-* specs, are in various states of acceptance. The Web Services Interoperability Organization (*http://www.ws-i.org*) was formed to provide a framework and a set of tools to ensure that different vendors' implementations of a particular WS-* spec are compatible.

For more information about the current Web services standards being defined and the location of the specifications, see *Web Services Specifications* on MSDN® (*http://msdn.microsoft.com/library/default.asp?url=/library/en-us/dnglobspec/html/wsspecsover.asp*).

## Extract, Transform, and Load

Extract, Transform, and Load (ETL) is a data integration technology that allows you to consolidate critical information from multiple enterprise data sources. Data is extracted and transformed to fit the data model of the target data store and is then loaded into that data store. ETL technologies are typically used to load high volumes of information into data warehouses and data marts from multiple databases.

## Communications Message Protocols

Communications message protocols, such as TCP/IP, HTTP, and FTP, define a standardized method of transport for messages exchanged between applications. They typically specify a standard set of headers as well as a way to package the content to be transported within the body of the message. Some protocols define the message headers for both the requests that the applications initiate and the corresponding responses. Your applications may use these protocols directly, or you may choose to build custom integration methods around the protocols.

## Screen Scraping

Sometimes the business logic of an application resides in the presentation layer. In this case, you can use software packages that simulate the human user's interactions to interface with the application. Screen scraping is a noninvasive mode of integration and does not introduce any additional channels of interface with the application. You can implement this technology in two ways:

- Use terminal emulation software to intercept screen images after they have been formatted into the terminal data stream.
- Intercept the data before it is formatted for display purposes. This method generally provides better performance and requires less interaction than using terminal emulation software.


You can use program calls to access the internal resources of an application. Applications supporting program calls are typically multitiered and modular, permitting external programs to take the place of the internal user interface layer of the application. They have a predefined set of inputs (parameters) and outputs (responses) depending on their business context. If you modify these inputs and outputs, you may also have to make corresponding modifications within the applications that are already invoking them.

## Direct Data Access

Direct data access involves making native database calls to application databases or writing data directly to the target application file systems. This approach requires knowledge of the data access language of the target database as well as knowledge of the data model used in the target application.

Direct updates to databases can make them vulnerable to data corruption and referential integrity violations. For this reason, many applications do not support direct data access. Instead, ordinarily you use their application programming interfaces (APIs) so that the calling programs can benefit from the business logic implemented within the applications.

## File Transfer

File transfer involves integration between multiple platforms through transfers of files in batch mode. Typically, you move data between systems asynchronously using batch file transfers, and the flow of data is unidirectional. Changes in one system rarely affect other systems unless the structure, format, or semantics of the data being moved changes. File transfer is a cost-effective solution for transferring batch files between a wide variety of platforms. A number of features add to the reliability and efficiency of file transfer, such as scheduling, automatic restart, guaranteed delivery, encryption/decryption, and compression/decompression.

## Human Involvement

Almost every integration environment still uses people to some extent. People may be involved in one or more of the following activities:

- **Presentation**. Presentation is the extraction and subsequent presentation of the information to be transferred through various media to a person. Presentation is accomplished through fax and e-mail messages, printouts, or visual display of the information on an application screen.

- **Validation**. People are sometimes required to visually inspect data to ensure that basic business rules are being followed. The validation process can be augmented by providing the people with a predefined set of valid values (for example, reference codes).

- **Transformation**. People are sometimes required to reformat or make semantic changes to the data without making changes to the basic content (for example, changing date formats or regrouping information across address fields to fix data entry errors).

- **Data entry**. Data entry is the act of reentering the data into the target application. Basic cut-and-paste techniques can be employed to minimize the time spent and errors incurred in the data entry process.

# Challenges of Application Integration

Application integration poses its own special difficulties, some technical and some organizational.

## Technical Issues

Because application integration is a relatively new area of IT for most organizations, often no single product resolves all application integration issues. Instead, an application integration environment usually consists of a series of technologies, including prepackaged and custom software applications.

When you build an application integration environment, you are creating an environment that allows components to communicate with each other even though they were never designed to do so. In many cases, these components are not even aware of each other. They may include a variety of preexisting systems (some of which are essential to your environment), packaged applications with proprietary APIs, geographically disbursed databases, and a variety of hardware, operating systems, and protocols. Yet your environment needs to be noninvasive to existing applications. In these conditions, complex architectural issues such as the following can arise:

- Control and coupling
- Data exchange and data formats
- Distribution and concurrency
- Scalability, reliability, and availability

Some of the most significant technical challenges of designing an application integration environment involve identifying the technical needs for your solution and determining the combination of products and services that will provide for those needs. Because this segment of the market is still evolving rapidly, you should pay particular attention to the maturity of integration technologies, methodologies, and standards. You do not want to completely rebuild the application integration environment itself every few months. The aim, instead, is to have a relatively stable application integration environment, which is flexible enough to allow the addition of new applications or the alteration of relationships between applications.

Organizational issues in application integration arise mainly from the fact that your application integration environment will span multiple departments in your organization. Staff in different departments may choose to deploy applications that will then need to integrate with the rest of your environment. To design a truly effective application integration environment, you need to isolate application integration as a separate management function, and determine who is responsible for making it happen. In larger organizations, you may have a group of people specifically responsible for this function, including application integration architects, application architects, and application owners, whereas in other cases, application integration may be one of many management functions that you are responsible for. Either way, by defining the application integration management function in this way, you help to ensure that it is properly considered whenever changes are made to the IT infrastructure.

Establishing governance processes around application integration can be difficult, because the processes must encompass not only application integration, but also the end systems and business processes that are being integrated. In fact, during the deployment phase, you should be involved in defining the baseline infrastructure as well.

Organizational issues in application integration can be particularly tricky when you are working in a decentralized enterprise or in a business-to-business (B2B) scenario. However, these scenarios often have the greatest need for an effective application integration environment. Therefore, it is particularly important to resolve any organizational issues early on, so that you can focus on resolving the technical challenges of application integration.

## Summary

An effective application integration environment should solve the problems of integrating applications, without requiring an enterprise to standardize on one hardware platform, one group of applications, or one operating system. Effective integration allows you to make a heterogeneous approach work even as you modify the elements within the mix. This chapter examined the problems that an effective application integration environment addresses, and discussed some of the implementation choices for application integration. The next chapter discusses what you need from your application integration environment to solve business problems.

# 2

# Defining Your Application Integration Environment

At a simple level, application integration means helping a series of applications communicate with one another better. To ensure that the integration is both beneficial and feasible, however, you should closely examine the business processes that must be integrated before focusing on the applications themselves. If you understand the business processes that your organization uses, you can map those processes to your application integration requirements. This chapter discusses the different levels at which application integration can occur, and shows which capabilities your application integration environment may require at each level. It also examines some of the issues you are likely to face when creating your application integration environment.

## Levels of Application Integration

Application integration can occur at many different levels, including:

- Presentation level
- Business process level
- Data level
- Communications level

Presentation-level integration can be a very effective way of integrating applications in your environment. Presentation-level integration allows multiple applications to be presented as a single cohesive application, often using existing application user interfaces. This guide does not cover presentation-level integration in any detail.

The following paragraphs discuss the other forms of integration in more detail.

## Business Process – Level Integration

Business process–level integration often forms the starting point for defining your application integration environment, because it is most closely related to the business requirements of your organization. Business process–level integration starts with defining your business processes and then specifying the logical integration that corresponds to those processes.

### Defining Your Business Processes

Before you can design your application integration environment, it is important to understand your organization in logical terms, removed from the technology that underlies it. At this stage, you are not interested in whether information needs to travel from one computer to another using messaging, using file transfer, or using request/reply. Nor are you particularly interested in what protocols are used, or whether it is necessary to perform semantic mapping between two systems. Those considerations, and others, are necessary later, but first you need to define your business processes.

Business processes consist of a group of logical activities that model the activities in your organization. These activities typically represent the smallest units of logical work that can be done in your organization. A typical example of an activity is *Update Inventory*, which is invoked when new inventory arrives, or when a customer order is placed.

Business processes usually have a beginning and an ending state, and generally have action-oriented names. They perform work and can be measured while doing so. For example, the business process *Process Order* might represent a series of activities, including *Enter Order*, *Accept Payment*, *Schedule Production*, and *Update Inventory*. When the order is processed, it goes from an unprocessed state to a processed state. The order-processing rate can be measured to show the efficiency of the process.

Any applications that are related in a given business process are candidates for integration. The reason for integrating the applications is to help the business process in some way; by making it faster, less error-prone, or less expensive, for example.

As you define your business processes, you should consider the following factors:

- **Place**. Can the business process be completed in one location, either for the client or the business? If a change of location is required, the business process cannot be completed in one time interval, and its state must be stored.
- **Time**. Can the business process be completed in one interaction with the business, or does it need to wait for some events, meaning that it occurs over multiple time intervals? If it cannot be completed in one interval, for example due to legislation, then state must be stored.

These dimensions define the complexity of the business process. They also drive the complexity of the integration of IT services in terms of whether the IT service is available at that place and time, and whether the service has the necessary business process state information. The complexity of the business process can also be affected by the nature of the applications involved in integration; for example, their maturity, degree of integration, and so on.

## Business Process Modeling

Business process modeling consists of defining the logical processes in your environment, identifying the start and end points, and determining the logical path between those points. The models can be generated in text or in flowchart form.

You should use business process modeling to define the details of each of the business processes that occur in your organization. Some of the steps may currently be automated; others may represent manual processes. The more complete your models, the easier it is to design an application integration environment that closely matches the needs of your organization.

### Modeling Simple Business Processes

Some business processes are very simple. They consist of a single interaction with a business and are completed in a single time interval. Someone (for example, a customer or partner) or something (an automated request) contacts the business and makes a request. This request may be made through a member of staff, or through a self-service facility. For a typical simple business process, the organization has a process that can handle the request immediately, and the process closes. There is no need to save the state of the business process (although there may be a need to record the occurrence of event and the result). Examples of simple business processes include:

- Registering to use services on a Web site
- Requesting an inventory of goods of a particular type
- Asking for a quotation for a service

Business processes can be quite complex. They can occur over multiple time intervals and in multiple places, and they can require state information about the business process to be managed. Often the steps include a combination of automated and manual steps. Figure 2.1, on the next page, shows a model of a sample complex business process.

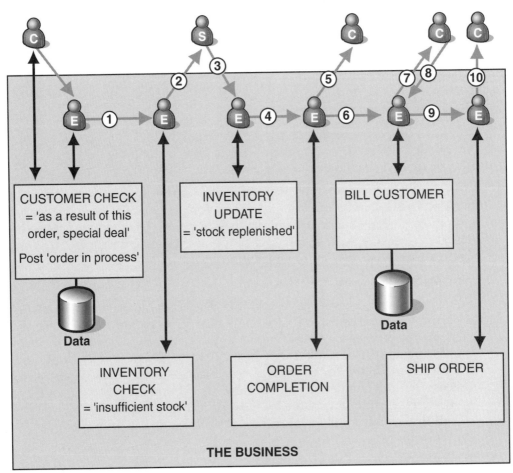

① Inventory and delivery?

② Supply and delivery?

③ Confirmed

④ Order can be met

⑤ Send notification

⑥ Bill using special terms

⑦ Send bill

⑧ Payment received

⑨ Send goods

⑩ Goods

**C** Customer   **S** Supplier   **E** Employee

**Figure 2.1**
*Model of a complex business process*

**Note:** The following description does not match the key in Figure 2.1, because the numbers in the figure define order processing steps that humans perform, while the following steps explain the entire business process.

The business process shown in Figure 2.1 consists of the following steps.

1. Someone (for example, a customer or partner) or something (an automated request) contacts the business and initiates an order for goods either through a self-service mechanism or through an order-entry representative of the business.

2. The Order Management system captures the order details. The system recognizes that this customer has placed enough orders with the company to qualify for a discount on the goods. The system includes this fact with the order information that it has gathered. The system marks the order in the database as 'order in process'.

3. The event originator is told that the order is under way and that progress updates will be coming.

4. A business staff member is aware of the order status (either because he or she is handling the order, or because he or she has received a notification from the external event handler IT service). This staff member initiates a request to check for inventory or delivery. This request is a person-to-person communication that may be initiated by e-mail, written note, or phone. Key details are passed to a staff member in the Inventory Management department.

5. The Inventory Management staff member checks that enough stock exists to fulfill the order. In this case, it does not, so the staff member issues a service request to a supplier for more stock and a promise of delivery date. This service request may be initiated by e-mail, paper form, or phone. The order details are not changed.

6. At some point, the supplier replies to Inventory Management. A staff member in the department updates the stock position in the supporting IT system. The staff member checks the orders waiting for inventory, finds the appropriate order, and then notifies the Order Management department that this order can now be fulfilled from stock on the date that the supplier has promised.

7. A staff member in Order Management updates the department database with this information, and issues a notice to the event originator confirming the order and the terms. Order Management passes the order information to the Billing department and asks Billing to issue the bill, using the new special terms.

8. Billing recalculates the bill, updates the billing database, and sends the bill to the customer. The bill notifies the customer that the goods will be shipped when payment has been received.

9. When Billing receives payment, a staff member updates the billing database and then notifies the Logistics department that the order can be shipped.

10. A staff member in Logistics schedules delivery and notifies the customer of when to expect the goods.

As this example suggests, a complex business process can be relatively difficult to model. Where you encounter problems in modeling a complex business process, you should break down any complex constituent processes into a number of simpler ones. Occasionally, however, the processes are so complex that it is impossible to model them accurately.

## Business Processing Standards

One advantage of business processes being entirely logical is that they have no dependence on the underlying technology. This enables you to define business processes according to predefined standards, which has the following benefits:

- You can interchange business processes more easily between organizations, with trading partners interacting at the process level rather than at the data level. This results in simpler business-to-business interaction.

- You can recruit individuals who are already familiar with the standards you have adopted.

- You can deploy software that has built-in support for those standards.

Existing business processing standards represent both the language and the visual representation of those processes. This allows you to define your business processes textually or visually, and then use tools to translate them into the corresponding language representation.

Business processes are most commonly represented by XML-based languages. The two most commonly used languages are Business Process Execution Language for Web Services (BPEL4WS) version 1.1 and Business Process Modeling Language (BPML) version 1.0.

The Business Process Modeling Notation (BPMN) version 1.0 specification, released by the Business Process Management Initiative (BPMI) Notation Working Group, allows both BPEL4WS 1.1 and BPML 1.0 to be represented using common elements. BPMN supports process management by providing a notation that is intuitive to business users and yet is able to represent complex process semantics.

## Mapping Business Requirements to Your Application Integration Requirements

After you have determined the business processes that your organization uses, you can begin to examine how they affect your application integration requirements. It is important to realize that a simple business process does not always correspond to simple requirements for application integration. In fact, a simple business process may require complex interaction between multiple applications.

Figure 2.2 shows a simple business process that requires the integration of multiple applications.

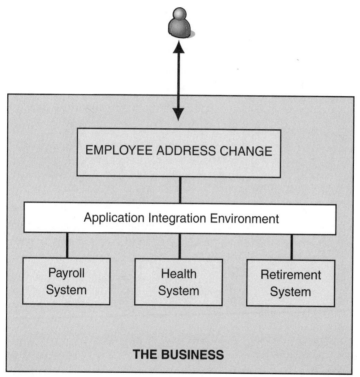

**Figure 2.2**

*Simple business process requiring application integration*

By modeling each of your business processes, you can define which applications must integrate with one another, and in what way. This enables you to make intelligent decisions about the specifics of your application integration environment.

## Business Processing Integration Capabilities

Table 2.1 shows a number of capabilities that are required for effective business processing integration.

**Table 2.1: Business Processing Capabilities**

| Capability | Description |
|---|---|
| Rules Processing | Allows you to define rules and process them at run time. |
| Business Transaction Management | Ensures that if a business activity fails, related activities are canceled. |
| Workflow | Controls the interaction between people and automated processes. |
| Orchestration | Coordinates the execution of the different activities that make up a business process. |
| State Management | Maintains the state in the context of pending applications. |
| Event Processing | Recognizes when business events have occurred, logs those events, and determines which business process capability receives the event. |
| Schedule | Generates events when a defined time period has elapsed or at a particular time of day. Also tracks processes in which an external event should occur within a specified time frame or by a specified date or time. |
| Contract Management | Monitors and processes contractual obligations at run time. |

For more information about each of these capabilities, see the Appendix, "Application Integration Capabilities."

# Data-Level Integration

You can define how applications communicate with each other at a business process level, but if they cannot understand the data they exchange, they cannot integrate successfully. Because different applications often handle data in different ways, a number of capabilities are required to establish integration at the data layer.

There are two general ways to enable data-level integration:

- Add logic to enable each application to understand incoming data from other applications.

- Add logic to enable each application to interpret outgoing data to an intermediate data format and interpret incoming data from that format into a form the application understands.

**Note:** In each case, the logic may modify the application itself or, more commonly, may place an interface in front of each application.

The problem with the first approach is common to most areas of application integration—a lack of scalability. In most enterprise situations, application integration architecture should instead adopt the second approach, with the data level using an intermediate data language.

Different integration scenarios have different data-level requirements. For example, if you synchronize data between two applications that store customer information, the data may need to be formatted to fit the data format of the target application. However, if the data is being moved into a data warehouse or data mart, the data may not only have to be formatted, but it may also have to be sorted, filtered, or otherwise processed so that it suits the needs of the users.

The nature of the applications you integrate may alter the way in which your data capabilities can function. For example, if you are moving data between applications in real time, the data-level capabilities generally work on one message at a time, and yet they may still need to support a very high volume of transactions per hour. To meet these needs, the data capabilities must normally be small, quick, and multithreaded. Other applications may only need to transfer data in batches (for example, loading a data warehouse every night at midnight). In this case, the data capabilities may not have to be multithreaded, but they may need to be particularly strong at sorting, summarizing, and filtering sets of data.

To support the various complex data integration requirements, your application integration solution must often contain a considerable amount of logic that supports the access, interpretation, and transformation of data. You also need schematic models of enterprise data to describe data attributes. The definition and recognition of schemas enables the validation of data. Descriptions of how data elements may be related or mapped to each other allow for the transformation of data.

## Data Integration Capabilities

Table 2.2 shows a number of capabilities that are required for effective data integration.

**Table 2.2: Data Integration Capabilities**

| Capability | Description |
|---|---|
| Data Transformation | Modifies the appearance or format of the data (without altering its content) so that applications can use it. |
| Data Validation | Determines whether data meets the predefined technical criteria. |
| Data Access | Determines how data is collected and presented to applications. |
| Schema Definition | Maintains predefined schemas. |
| Mapping | Manages the relationship between applications and determines how the data must be transformed from the source to the target application. |
| Schema Recognition | Checks that the schema can be read and understood, and that it is well-formed. |

For more information about each of these capabilities, see the Appendix, "Application Integration Capabilities."

# Communications-Level Integration

Although the forms of integration already discussed are very important, they all depend on integration at the communications level. Unless applications can communicate with each other, you cannot integrate them.

Not all applications are designed to communicate in the same way. Some communicate synchronously, others asynchronously. Some use file transfer to communicate; others interact through messaging or request/reply.

The nature of the applications you are integrating often determines how communications occur between them. Older applications may use file transfer for communications, and some may not be designed to communicate with other applications at all. Newer applications often use message-based communication and may use predefined standards to facilitate communication. Before determining the requirements for your communications-level integration, you need to examine the communication needs for your environment and the existing capabilities of your applications.

## Enabling Communication Between Applications

Because many applications are not designed to communicate directly with each other, it is likely that you will need to do some development work to ensure that your applications can be called by other applications.

There are two possible approaches to this problem:

- Rewrite your application to provide it with an API that other applications can call.
- Create a communications adaptor that acts as an intermediary between the application and other applications.

Although rewriting an application to add APIs may seem like a more elegant solution than creating a series of bolted-on connectors or adapters, the time, effort, and risk associated with rewriting older applications makes the connector approach a preferred solution in most circumstances. However, for widely distributed and diverse applications, the distribution and management of connectors can generate significant management overhead.

You also need to determine whether the communication between applications will occur directly on a point-to-point basis, or through an intermediary hub. For more information, see "Making Application Integration Scalable" in Chapter 1, "Introduction."

## Communications-Level Capabilities

Table 2.3 shows a number of capabilities that are required for effective communications integration.

**Table 2.3: Communications Capabilities**

| Capability | Description |
|---|---|
| Message Routing | Controls the routing of messages from the source to the target application. |
| Message Delivery | Determines how messages pass from the source application to the target application. |
| Message Queuing | Implements reliable messaging. |
| Message Forwarding | Provides serial message handling. |
| Message Correlation | Ensures that reply messages are matched to request messages. |
| Message Instrumentation | Ensures that the messages are processed in the order that was originally intended. |
| Addressing | Determines where messages should be sent. |
| Transactional Delivery | Groups together messages, sending and receiving them within a transaction. |
| File Transfer | Moves files between applications. |
| Serialization/Deserialization | Converts data to and from a flat structure to send it over the network. |

*(continued)*

| Capability | Description |
|---|---|
| Request/Reply | Waits on a request sent to the target until a response is received. |
| Batching/Unbatching | Collects messages together for transmission and separates them at the destination. |
| Encode/Decode | Ensures that applications using different encoding methods or code pages can communicate. |
| Connection Management | Establishes a logical connection between applications in a request/reply scenario. |

Not all of these capabilities are required for every application integration scenario. This guide discusses how to determine which capabilities are required in your environment.

**Note:** For a more detailed description of each capability, see the Appendix, "Application Integration Capabilities."

# Important Considerations for Application Integration

The specifics of your application integration environment depend on many things, including the complexity of both your business processes and your IT environment. Several considerations, however, are common to many application integration environments. This section discusses these issues.

**Note:** For more details about the specific capabilities that are required for an application integration environment, see the Appendix, "Application Integration Capabilities."

## Using Synchronous and Asynchronous Communication

One important consideration in an application integration environment is how the applications communicate with each other. They may use synchronous or asynchronous communication, or most commonly, a combination of the two.

Often the applications themselves determine the best forms of communication to use. In situations where the application must wait for a reply before it continues processing, synchronous communication is often most appropriate. Asynchronous communication is normally appropriate in situations where the application can continue processing after it sends a message to the target application.

Just considering the needs of the application may be a too simplistic way of determining whether to use synchronous or asynchronous communication, however. Communication may be synchronous at the application level, for example, but the underlying architecture that enables this connectivity may be asynchronous.

Generally, a number of capabilities are required to support synchronous and asynchronous communication. Table 2.4 shows these capabilities.

**Table 2.4: Capabilities Used in Synchronous and Asynchronous Communication**

| Form of communication | Capabilities required |
|---|---|
| Synchronous communication | Request/Reply<br>Connection Management |
| Asynchronous communication | Message Routing<br>Addressing<br>Message Forwarding<br>Message Delivery<br>Message Queuing<br>Message Instrumentation<br>Message Correlation |

Asynchronous communication offers a potential performance advantage, because applications are not continually waiting for a response and then timing out when they do not receive one in a timely fashion. Asynchronous communication offers other performance benefits as well. Because asynchronous communication is connectionless, a continuous link is not maintained between each side of a data exchange. This arrangement can provide a small performance advantage over connection-based communications, and may also reduce the load on the network. However, any advantage may be offset, at least in part, by a need to match replies to initial messages at the application level. Using the Message Queuing capability to ensure message delivery can also diminish performance.

Although applications traditionally rely on synchronous communications, applications can maintain the same functionality while taking advantage of the benefits of asynchronous communications. In most cases, you should design your application integration environment to support both synchronous and asynchronous communication, because more often than not, both will be required. However, you should consider adopting an asynchronous model for communications whenever possible.

## Increasing Automation

One of the most significant aims of an application integration environment is to reduce the amount of human involvement in integrating applications, and therefore to move increasingly towards fully automated application integration. Of course, in many cases this is not possible. However, it is likely that some of your organization's business processes can be more automated.

In particular, you may have many applications that enable you to perform business processes, but that require a series of manual steps. Manual steps might include interacting with a number of applications consecutively. As an example, if a staff member named Bob orders 100 widgets from the Manufacturing department, the business process might resemble the following.

1. Bob chooses the widgets in an online catalog.
2. Bob creates a purchase order for the widgets.
3. Bob sends the purchase order to his manager for approval.
4. Bob's manager approves the purchase and sends a copy of the approved purchase order to the Finance department. Finance stores the purchase order as a pending purchase.
5. Bob sends the purchase order to the Manufacturing department, copying Finance so they know the purchase has been made. Finance stores the purchase order as an outstanding purchase.
6. Manufacturing sends the widgets, updates its inventory, and invoices Finance for the purchase amount.
7. Finance transfers the money to the widgets manufacturing department.

The previous example uses a series of applications in a specific order. Much of this processing can be automated so that applications interact with each other. For example, by integrating the online catalog with the application creating the purchase order, you can save Bob a step and save the company some money. Actually, this type of process can be completely automated (with pauses for human approval). Some of the steps are sequential, but others can be performed in parallel (for example, Finance can store the purchase order as an outstanding purchase as Manufacturing sends the widgets). The order of events depends on the overall nature of the business process.

## Straight-Through Processing (STP)

Some business transactions do not require any human intervention. The processing for such transactions is known as straight-through processing (STP). The goals of using STP include:

- Improving customer service by reducing the opportunity for human errors and by speeding up the business process handoffs.
- Reducing the cost of the business process through automation that results in lower staff costs.
- Reducing batch processing.

A single business transaction often involves multiple applications working in conjunction with each other, and in this case your application integration environment must provide the logic that would otherwise be provided by people. This is achieved by defining business rules for the transaction to follow.

Figure 2.3 shows straight-through processing occurring with multiple applications.

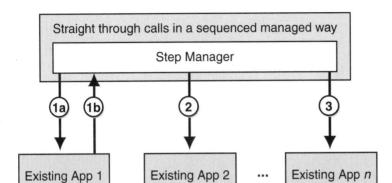

**Figure 2.3**
*Straight-through processing with multiple applications*

Your decision on how extensively you use STP normally involves a tradeoff between initial costs and benefits. Dramatically reducing the amount of human interaction in your business processes can involve the creation of some very complex business logic and similarly complex IT solutions. You need to determine at what point the development costs exceed the benefits of extra automation.

### Business Processing Capabilities Used in STP

Business processing capabilities are frequently used to provide straight-through processing. The only capability that is not generally used is the Workflow capability, because it normally applies to situations that require human interaction with the system. Table 2.5 summarizes the business processing capabilities used in STP.

**Table 2.5: Business Processing Capabilities Used in STP**

| Capability | Usage |
| --- | --- |
| Rules Processing | Normally used |
| Business Transaction Management | Normally used |
| Workflow | Not used |
| Orchestration | Normally used |
| State Management | Normally used |
| Event Processing | Normally used |
| Schedule | Normally used |
| Contract Management | Normally used |

### Data Capabilities Used in STP

Some data capabilities are essential for STP, but others are used only in specific situations. When the structure and format of data differs across the applications involved in STP, you need the Data Transformation and/or Mapping capabilities. If the flow is between different business domains, but within the same application working with the same data formats, you generally do not need these capabilities.

You may need the Data Access capability if the end-to-end response time of STP is unacceptable. By deploying the Data Access capability, you can ensure that data is staged for faster access, which should improve the overall performance of STP. If the overall response time is acceptable as is, you do not need the Data Access capability.

Table 2.6 summarizes the data capabilities used in STP.

**Table 2.6: Data Capabilities Used in STP**

| Capability | Usage |
|---|---|
| Data Transformation | Sometimes used |
| Data Validation | Normally used |
| Data Access | Sometimes used |
| Schema Definition | Normally used |
| Mapping | Sometimes used |
| Schema Recognition | Normally used |

### Communications Capabilities Used in STP

Some communications capabilities are essential for STP. Others are used only in specific situations, and some should not be used at all. STP usually uses a messaging style of communication throughout the business process. This means that the messaging capabilities are generally required, but capabilities such as Request/Reply, Connection Management, Batching/Unbatching, and File Transfer are not. However, Request/Reply and Connection Management are useful for implementing some work-step invocation and response. File Transfer, while it is not the optimal solution, can be used as an alternative to messaging if your communications environment is based on file transfer.

The Message Forwarding capability enables indirect access to applications. This capability is normally not required in STP, which involves a concrete set of applications that are directly accessed. If you do need access to additional applications, you can make these applications part of the STP flow so that they do not require Message Forwarding.

Transactional Delivery is not always required for STP. Transactional Delivery is necessary in situations where multiple messages must be processed together or not processed at all through the constituent steps of a given STP flow. However, many STP flows do not necessarily involve such grouping of messages. Therefore, you should examine the specifics of your STP environment to determine if you need Transactional Delivery.

Serialization/Deserialization may be required if the structure of the data is very different across the applications that are part of the overall flow. If the flow is between different business domains within the same application working with the same data structures, Serialization/Deserialization is not necessary.

If the applications in the STP flow exist on different operating systems or represent data in different languages, you may require the Encode/Decode capability. Otherwise it is not normally needed.

Table 2.7 summarizes the communications capabilities used in STP.

**Table 2.7: Communications Capabilities Used in STP**

| Capability | Usage |
| --- | --- |
| Message Routing | Normally used |
| Message Delivery | Normally used |
| Message Queuing | Normally used |
| Message Forwarding | Not used |
| Message Correlation | Normally used |
| Message Instrumentation | Normally used |
| Addressing | Normally used |
| Transactional Delivery | Sometimes used |
| File Transfer | Sometimes used |
| Serialization/Deserialization | Sometimes used |
| Request/Reply | Sometimes used |
| Batching/Unbatching | Not used |
| Encode/Decode | Sometimes used |
| Connection Management | Sometimes used |

## Ensuring Data Integrity

In any application integration environment, data is generally passed from one location to another. In some cases, a master writable copy of the data exists, and other applications read from and write to that location. In such cases, your application integration environment needs to support only basic data replication. In other cases, however, multiple writable copies of the data exist. This data may exist in multiple databases, formats, and locations, and on multiple platforms. However, you still must maintain data integrity in each location.

To maintain data integrity in your environment, you should consider the amount and complexity of data that you are storing. You may have multiple writable copies of data in situations where a single master copy is more appropriate. Or maybe the format of your data can be standardized across your organization. Examining the data integrity requirements of your organization before building your application integration environment can save you a lot of money.

As an example of a data integrity problem, imagine that your company maintains employee information in multiple databases. The number of vacation days allowed for your employees exists in a human resources database, but salary information resides in a financial database. Both of these databases contain a record for each employee, but the records are separate. If you want to examine all of the records for an employee named Smith, you must retrieve records from both databases. If Smith marries and changes her name to Jones, you must modify records in each database to ensure that both are correct.

### Data Synchronization

You can ensure that data integrity is maintained in your organization by using the data synchronization capabilities of your application integration environment.

Data synchronization is the act of reconciling the contents of two or more databases to bring them into an agreed-upon state of consistency, according to agreed-upon rules. Data synchronization is (at any one time) one-way, because data is changed in one location and is then copied out to other locations that require it. Depending on the requirements, the data may be copied when a particular event occurs, or at a particular time.

In a data synchronization environment, it is not generally practical for each program that changes one instance of common data to change all other instances. Instead, the data synchronization logic normally propagates the changes to the other copies at some later time. This behavior can lead to data concurrency issues. For more information about concurrency, see "Managing Latency" later in this chapter.

**Note:** Data synchronization between two applications is often required in both directions. However, in these cases synchronization actually consists of two one-way processes rather than one two-way process.

Figure 2.4 illustrates data synchronization between two applications.

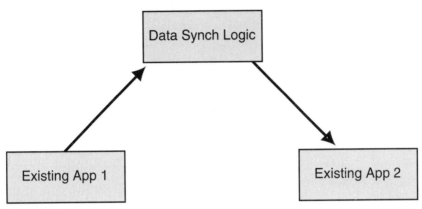

**Figure 2.4**
*Data synchronization between two applications*

### Business Processing Capabilities Used in Data Synchronization

The Rules Processing and Business Transaction Management capabilities are normally required for data synchronization. Rules Processing is required to validate the data. Business Transaction Management is required because data must be synchronized across all databases or none of them. All of the other business processing capabilities, however, are either sometimes used or not used at all.

The Workflow, Event Processing, and Schedule capabilities may be required, depending on the specifics of your environment. The Workflow capability is used when business users have to choose between duplicate instances of the same entity (for example, multiple addresses for the same person) during the synchronization process. Event Processing is required when synchronization depends on a given event (for example, the sale of a product registered on a point-of-sale device, which initiates a purchase order on the manufacturer's order entry system). The Schedule capability is used when synchronization must occur at a given time.

Table 2.8 summarizes the business processing capabilities used in data synchronization.

**Table 2.8: Business Processing Capabilities Used in Data Synchronization**

| Capability | Usage |
|---|---|
| Rules Processing | Normally used |
| Business Transaction Management | Normally used |
| Workflow | Sometimes used |
| Orchestration | Not used |
| State Management | Not used |
| Event Processing | Sometimes used |
| Schedule | Sometimes used |
| Contract Management | Not used |

### Data Capabilities Used in Data Synchronization

As you would expect, data synchronization uses many of the data capabilities. The only capabilities that you may not need to implement are the Mapping and Data Transformation capabilities. Often, you do not need these capabilities, for example if data is synchronized across relational databases on a single platform that stores enterprise-level data in a consistent structure and format. You should examine the applications, platforms, and data involved in synchronization to determine the need for data transformation and mapping in your environment.

Table 2.9 summarizes the data capabilities used in data synchronization.

**Table 2.9: Data Capabilities Used in Data Synchronization**

| Capability | Usage |
|---|---|
| Data Transformation | Sometimes used |
| Data Validation | Normally used |
| Data Access | Normally used |
| Schema Definition | Normally used |
| Mapping | Sometimes used |
| Schema Recognition | Normally used |

### Communications Capabilities Used in Data Synchronization

Some communications capabilities are essential for data synchronization. Others are used only in specific situations, and some should not be used at all.

Data synchronization is, by definition, one-way. Even in situations where it appears to be bidirectional, you can think of it as two one-way processes. For this reason,

Request/Reply, Connection Management, and Message Correlation normally are not used in data synchronization. Message Instrumentation is not used, because messages do not need to be processed in a predefined sequence. Message Forwarding is not used either, because data synchronization occurs directly with each database instance.

Other messaging capabilities are typically used as a means of communication for data synchronization. File Transfer may also be used for data synchronization. You will often decide whether to use File Transfer based on the capabilities of the applications involved and on the availability of other communications capabilities.

Serialization/Deserialization may be required if the structure of the data is very different in the databases that are being synchronized.

Synchronization usually applies to a given instance of a business entity. However, you may use the Batching/Unbatching capability to update a logical set of data records (for example, customer records and all the associated address records). Or you may use it to batch the records together for performance reasons.

You may require the Encode/Decode capability if the databases to be synchronized exist on different operating systems or represent data in different languages. Otherwise, it is not normally needed.

Table 2.10 summarizes the communications capabilities used in data synchronization.

**Table 2.10: Communications Capabilities Used in Data Synchronization**

| Capability | Usage |
|---|---|
| Message Routing | Normally used |
| Message Delivery | Normally used |
| Message Queuing | Normally used |
| Message Forwarding | Not used |
| Message Correlation | Not used |
| Message Instrumentation | Not used |
| Addressing | Normally used |
| Transactional Delivery | Normally used |
| File Transfer | Sometimes used |
| Serialization/Deserialization | Sometimes used |
| Request/Reply | Not used |
| Batching/Unbatching | Sometimes used |
| Encode/Decode | Sometimes used |
| Connection Management | Not used |

## Managing Latency

If you have multiple sources of data, it will not be identical in all locations at all times. There will be a delay between the time that information is written in one location and the time that those changes are reflected in other locations. Your business requirements will determine what kind of time delay is acceptable.

As an example, imagine that your business provides services to your customers for a monthly fee. However, a customer has a complaint, and as a courtesy, you agree to reduce the cost of your services by 10 percent. This information is fed into your customer relationship management (CRM) database. However, in order for it to be reflected in the bill, the information must be synchronized with the billing database. In this case, the information must be in the billing database before the bills are issued, which could be in several days. However, if billing information is available immediately to the customer on the Web, you may need to ensure that the updates occur within minutes.

### Concurrency Issues

Latency in the updating of data can cause significant problems, especially if the same record is updated in multiple locations. You must ensure that when these delays occur the resultant data is consistent and correct.

Consider the following approaches to maintaining data concurrency:

- Pessimistic concurrency
- Optimistic concurrency
- Business actions and journals

The following paragraphs discuss each approach in turn.

#### Pessimistic Concurrency

Pessimistic concurrency assumes that if one instance of data is updated from multiple sources, the desired result will not occur; therefore, it prevents such attempts. In such cases, each time a user attempts to modify the database, the database is locked until the change is complete. Pessimistic concurrency can be problematic, because a single user, or client, may hold a lock for a significant period of time. It could involve locking resources such as database rows and files, or holding onto resources such as memory and connections. However, pessimistic concurrency may be appropriate where you have complete control over how long resources will be locked.

#### Optimistic Concurrency

Optimistic concurrency assumes that any particular update will produce the desired result, but provides information to verify the result. When an update request is submitted, the original data is sent along with the changed data. The original data is checked to see if it still matches the current data in its own store (normally the database). If it does, the update is executed; otherwise, the request is denied, producing an optimistic failure. To optimize the process, you can use a time stamp or an update counter in the data, in which case only the time stamp needs to be checked. Optimistic concurrency provides a good mechanism for updating master data that does not change very often, such as a customer's phone number. Optimistic concurrency allows everyone to read; and because updates are rare, the chance of running into an optimistic failure is minimal. Optimistic concurrency is not an efficient method to use in situations where the transactions are likely to fail often.

### Business Actions and Journals

For situations in which data changes frequently, one of the most useful methods for achieving concurrency is to use business actions and journals. This approach relies on standard bookkeeping techniques. You simply record changes to the data in separate debit and credit fields.

For example, imagine that your company provides widgets for customers. The company receives two requests that alter the field containing the number of widgets. One request is a return of 20 widgets, and the other is a sale of 20 widgets. If you use business actions and journals, both requests can be received, and the field does not need to be locked.

In fact, this approach does not require the locking of fields even for an order change. For example, suppose that the customer changes an order from 20 widgets to 11 widgets. This could be thought of as a single change, but it could also be thought of as two separate changes — first an order of 20 widgets, and then a return of 9 widgets.

This type of data concurrency approach may involve updating each record on the fly any time a change occurs, or it may involve posting the information into a journal, which is checked for consistency and completeness before all of the postings are executed.

Business actions and journals do not prevent optimistic failures entirely. For example, if an update request uses previously retrieved information (for example, the price of a widget), the retrieved information may be outdated and may require validation within the update operation. Your design should specify what must happen when such an optimistic exception occurs, because you may not always want to notify the user of such an exception.

One other problem with business actions and journals is the potential for a modification to be processed twice. Two orders for 20 widgets is obviously different from one order for 20 widgets. If business actions and journals are not used and the master data is modified directly, the widget inventory field can be changed from 200 widgets to 180 widgets multiple times, and it will make no difference. Therefore, if your application integration environment uses business actions and journals, it must also ensure that each action occurs once and only once.

## Data Aggregation

Some data must be merged together before it can be sent to other applications. For example, data may need to be combined from multiple applications, or from a single application over time.

The precise challenges of data aggregation depend on the number of records you are aggregating. Aggregation may take place one record at a time, or you may batch multiple records together to create one output message. Scaling up further, some batch integration solutions require the aggregation of thousands or even millions of records from dozens of applications. The processing requirements of data aggregation increase unpredictably as the number of input records grows to these levels. Consequently, a solution that works effectively for transactional data aggregation may not be able to keep up with batch data aggregation requirements. Therefore, in some cases you may need two separate data aggregation services—one optimized for smaller payloads and high transaction rates and a second service optimized for the batch processing of very large data sets.

Data aggregation can be particularly complex when different types of data arrive at the transformation service at different and unpredictable rates. An example is the merging of video and audio input, which requires synchronization over time. The solution often involves the use of temporary storage for data that must be synchronized with data that has not arrived yet.

# Combining Application Functionality

Many IT applications require user input from presentation devices. The interactions are designed to suit human needs and often to support conversations with customers. However, as you move to a more service-oriented architecture, you will find that applications have different requirements, particularly to support semantically rich messages.

In most cases, it does not make economic sense to completely create your new applications from scratch. Often someone has already built some of the functionality of the application for you, and if you know that the functionality works, you can use it to build reliable applications cheaper and more quickly. You can build the new application by adding new programming logic to existing building blocks of functionality.

## Application Composition

Application composition describes the functionality required to interpret messages from applications, make calls to other applications, extract relevant information from their replies, and pass the information back to the application that made the original request.

Composed applications have the following attributes:

- Interaction between components is synchronous and two-way.
- Interaction between components is fast, because a client application or user is waiting for a response.
- As data is updated in one component, it is updated in other dependent components.

Figure 2.5 shows an example of a composed application.

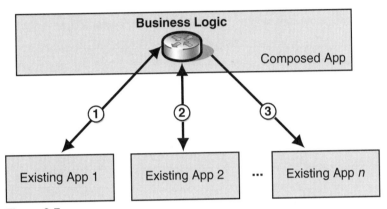

**Figure 2.5**
*A composed application*

A composed application often provides the same functionality from a business perspective as STP. Which option you choose depends on how costly the implementation is in the short term, the medium term, and the long term.

### Business Processing Capabilities Used in Application Composition

The Rules Processing capability is often used in application composition, because composed applications usually consist of reusable application components that contain business rules. Other capabilities may be used depending on the specifics of your environment.

The Business Transaction Management capability is often used to ensure that a complete transaction is successfully executed across all of the components in a composed application, but it is not needed in situations where a composed application does not have direct transactional responsibility (for example, in rules engines). The Workflow capability is required only in situations that involve human interaction. The State Management capability is used when application components have to resume processing after being in a suspended state.

Composed applications do not ordinarily rely on the Orchestration capability for multistep processing because orchestration logic is inherently embedded in the composed application. The Event Processing capability may also be built into composed applications; in fact, it is required for composed applications built out of silo applications, because it provides a mechanism for loosely coupled integration.

Composed applications do not use the Schedule capability because the communication is synchronous and two-way. Nor do they use the Contract Management capability. While contracts can exist between the application components that constitute a composed application, the management of those contracts is not related to the composed applications themselves.

Table 2.11 summarizes the capabilities needed to provide application composition.

**Table 2.11: Business Processing Capabilities Used in Application Composition**

| Capability | Usage |
|---|---|
| Rules Processing | Normally used |
| Business Transaction Management | Sometimes used |
| Workflow | Sometimes used |
| Orchestration | Sometimes used |
| State Management | Sometimes used |
| Event Processing | Sometimes used |
| Schedule | Not used |
| Contract Management | Not used |

### Data Capabilities Used In Application Composition

In a composed application, there is no guarantee of the quality and state of the inputs received by the individual application components. Therefore, the composed application components must use the Data Validation and Schema Recognition capabilities to validate the inputs they receive.

Other capabilities may be required, depending on the specifics of your environment. Usually, composed applications are built from modular, reusable building blocks of functionality with generic inputs and outputs that conform to the same semantic definition. In such scenarios, the Data Mapping and Data Transformation capabilities are not required. However, if applications are composed across platforms, or if the components are extended into application domains for which they were not originally designed, Data Mapping and/or Data Transformation are likely to be needed.

Schema Definition is required at the entry point of a composed application, and in some cases the individual components need to use the Schema Definition capability. In other cases, the composed applications may be built across multiple reusable components that recognize a single schema. Finally, in situations where you require better end-to-end response times in your composed application, you may need the Data Access capability to stage data for faster access.

Table 2.12 summarizes the data capabilities used in application composition.

**Table 2.12: Data Capabilities Used in Application Composition**

| Capability | Usage |
|---|---|
| Data Transformation | Sometimes used |
| Data Validation | Normally used |
| Data Access | Sometimes used |
| Schema Definition | Sometimes used |
| Mapping | Sometimes used |
| Schema Recognition | Normally used |

### Communications Capabilities Used in Application Composition

Because composed applications use synchronous two-way communication, the capabilities used to support this communication are generally required, including Request/Reply and Connection Management. However, as mentioned earlier in this chapter, communication that is synchronous from the perspective of the application may actually be asynchronous at the communications level. In these situations, the Addressing capability is required to directly address the constituent components of the application, and the Message Delivery capability is used to provide a single casting delivery mechanism between the different components of the composed application. The Message Correlation capability is also required to match messages to replies.

Several capabilities are not used at all for application composition. Given the real-time nature of the interactions between the components of a composed application, File Transfer, Batching/Unbatching, and Message Queuing are not used. With no Message Queuing, there is no need for the Transactional Delivery capability. Message Instrumentation is not used, because the entry-point application that invokes the components of a composed application ensures that messages are processed in the proper sequence.

Other capabilities are used only in certain circumstances. For example, Message Routing is usually not required because composed applications ordinarily follow a predefined sequence of steps that use the functionality already available within the application. However, the capability is required in cases where the business needs to modify this sequence in a way that is not supported by the application.

In situations where components of a composed application represent multiple applications, you can use the Message Forwarding capability to ensure that each application receives the information it requires.

The Serialization/Deserialization capability may be required if the structure of the data is very different across the composed application components. Similarly, the Encode/Decode capability may be needed if the composed application consists of components that reside on different operating systems.

Table 2.13 summarizes the communications capabilities used in application composition.

**Table 2.13: Communications Capabilities Used in Application Composition**

| Capability | Usage |
| --- | --- |
| Message Routing | Sometimes used |
| Message Delivery | Normally used |
| Message Queuing | Not used |
| Message Forwarding | Sometimes used |
| Message Correlation | Normally used |
| Message Instrumentation | Not used |
| Addressing | Normally used |
| Transactional Delivery | Not used |
| File Transfer | Not used |
| Serialization/Deserialization | Sometimes used |
| Request/Reply | Normally used |
| Batching/Unbatching | Not used |
| Encode/Decode | Sometimes used |
| Connection Management | Normally used |

## Managing Transactions

Managing transactions is challenging in any complex business environment because business processes do not consist of isolated activities. Instead, they consist of a series of related, interdependent activities. As you define your application integration environment, you need to include capabilities that help you manage transactions effectively.

Business applications are frequently required to coordinate multiple pieces of work as part of a single business transaction. For example, when you order goods online, your credit card is verified, you are billed, the goods are selected, boxed, and shipped, and inventory must be managed. All of these steps are interrelated, and if one step fails, all corresponding steps must be canceled as well.

Not only do you need to provide Business Transaction Management capabilities at the business process level, you also need to consider what happens at other levels of integration. Messages that pass between applications may also need to be passed as transactions to ensure that the system can roll back, in case one of a group of interrelated messages is not received properly.

Your application integration environment will normally include the following two capabilities to support transaction management:

- **Transactional Delivery**. A communications capability that ensures that transactions satisfy Atomicity, Consistency, Isolation, and Durability (ACID) requirements.

- **Business Transaction Management**. A business processing capability that ensures that when a transaction fails, the business can react appropriately, either by rolling back to the original state, or by issuing additional compensating transactions.

## Providing ACID Transactions

Traditionally, transaction management has been thought of in terms of ensuring that transactions meet the Atomicity, Consistency, Isolation, and Durability (ACID) requirements, which are defined as follows:

- *Atomicity* refers to the need to complete all the parts of the transaction or none of them. For example, when a pick list is generated to take a book from the shelf, the inventory quantity for that book should be decreased.

- *Consistency* refers to the need to maintain internal consistency among related pieces of data. For example, in a funds transfer application in a bank, a $100 withdrawal from a customer's savings account should be completed successfully only if a corresponding $100 deposit is made in that customer's checking account.

- *Isolation* refers to the need to ensure that the activities within one transaction are not mixed with the actions of parallel transactions. For example, if five simultaneous requests for a particular book arrive and the warehouse has only four copies of the book in stock, the five transactions must each run in isolation so that the orders are processed properly. Otherwise, it might be possible for each of the five business transactions to see an inventory level of five books and then try to reduce the number to four.

- *Durability* refers to the need to ensure that the results of the transaction are changed only by another valid transaction. The results of the transaction should not be compromised by a power outage or system failure.

When an atomic transaction runs, either all of its steps must be completed successfully or none of them should be completed. In other words, when a transaction failure occurs, the underlying applications and data should be returned to the exact state they were in before the failed transaction started.

Developing an application that satisfies these ACID requirements can be extremely complex, and the resulting application can be hard to scale. To streamline application development and to ensure scalability, software vendors offer transaction management software that is designed to satisfy the ACID requirements. This software generally takes one of two forms:

- **Database management systems**. Most enterprise-level database management systems provide transaction-processing features. Multiple applications can update multiple database tables or segments within a single, automatically managed transaction.

- **Transaction processing managers**. When data has to be updated on several databases or file systems on several diverse hardware or software platforms, a transaction processing manager can coordinate all of these actions within a single business transaction. This coordination saves you the task of writing an application to manage and coordinate the updates to each of these data sources.

Transaction processing managers generally conform to a set of standards called XA standards, which are governed by the Open Group (*www.opengroup.org*). In an XA-compliant distributed transaction management environment, a single transaction-processing manager coordinates the actions of multiple XA-compliant resource managers. A database, messaging system, file management system, or any runtime application environment can act as an XA-compliant resource manager as long it is able to perform the required transaction management tasks.

Transaction-processing managers can require significant processing power, high network bandwidth, and good management tools. Performance issues with transaction management are mostly associated with resource locking and communications overhead (for all of the extra communications traffic required to coordinate the highly dispersed transaction components).

## Transactional Messaging

Transactional messaging is used when you want to perform several tasks so that all tasks, including non-Message Queuing operations, either all succeed or all fail. When you use transactional messaging, the sending or receiving application has the opportunity to commit to the transaction (when all the operations have succeeded), or to abort the transaction (when at least one of the operations failed) so all changes are rolled back.

In Message Queuing, a single transaction can encompass multiple sending and receiving operations. However, the same message cannot be sent and received within a single transaction. In a case where a transaction consists of sending multiple messages, either all of the messages are transmitted in the order in which they were sent (if the transaction is committed), or none of the messages are transmitted (if the transaction is aborted). If multiple messages are sent to the same queue, Message Queuing guarantees that they arrive in the destination queue exactly once and in the order in which they were sent within the transaction.

Messages that are to be delivered in the order in which they were sent belong to the same *message stream*. Each message in a stream carries a *sequence number*, identifying its order in the stream, and a *previous number*, which equals the sequence number of the previous message in the stream. The message whose sequence number equals the previous number of another message must be present in the destination queue before the message can be delivered. The first message in a stream always carries a previous number equal to zero.

A transaction can also consist of removing multiple messages from a queue. The messages are removed from the queue only if and when the transaction is committed; otherwise, they are returned to the queue and can be subsequently read during another transaction.

Transactional messaging is slower than nontransactional messaging because messages are written to disk more than once and greater computer resources are required. Transactional messages can be sent only to transactional queues on the local computer or a remote computer. When messages are received within a transaction, they can be retrieved only from a local transactional queue. However, messages can be retrieved in nontransactional operations from local and remote transactional queues.

## Two-Phase Commit

Satisfying ACID requirements can be problematic if the components of the transaction are dispersed over some combination of multiple databases and transaction processing managers. ACID requirements are even harder to maintain when parts of the transaction are executed under the control of separate operational entities (for example, separate business units of a single enterprise or separate enterprises).

To satisfy ACID requirements in these environments, XA-compliant resource managers can control a two-phase commit. In a two-phase commit, the transaction processing manager first instructs each resource manager to prepare to commit. At that point, each resource manager writes the transaction's data to the database, file, or queue, but retains the data in memory. After all of the participating resource managers have successfully prepared to commit, the transaction processing manager issues a commit instruction. This is the second phase of the two-phase commit.

A two-phase commit is an extremely effective approach to satisfying the ACID requirements when different data stores and messaging systems must be coordinated. However, it is resource-intensive, with a lot of network traffic and a lot of interdependent system locks on pending local transactions. If an application or service is waiting for a reply and cannot continue until the reply is received, this approach can block business processes. A two-phase commit is appropriate for environments where each system is local to each other system; however, more distributed environments, particularly those using asynchronous transactions, require a different approach.

## Transaction Compensation

When applications are loosely coupled through asynchronous transactions, a two-phase commit usually becomes too problematic to implement because the atomicity of the transaction is difficult to maintain. In these situations, you can instead adopt an approach where compensating transactions are used to restore order when only part of a transaction is completed successfully.

As an example, consider a customer who is planning a vacation. When arranging the vacation, the customer must ensure availability of air travel, hotel, and rental car for the same week in the same location. If any one of these travel services cannot be arranged for that week in that place, then the entire transaction should be canceled.

For a tightly coupled transaction, the composite application has to contact the airline, hotel, and car rental reservation systems and keep each of them pending until all three can agree on a particular week. Because those activities may tie up transactions in the three reservation systems to an unacceptable degree, a better approach may be to handle this process as three individual transactions. In this case, if one or more actions cannot be completed, the other actions are canceled by executing a compensating transaction. Therefore, if the airline and car rental transactions are completed successfully, but the hotel reservation fails, then the composite application sends messages to the airline and car reservation systems to cancel those reservations. The composite application can then start over and look at availability for a different week or at a different resort.

The management of the logic required to recognize complete and incomplete distributed transactions and to issue compensating transactions is difficult to automate because each scenario can require different compensation strategies. Consequently, the process management capabilities of this integration architecture must readily enable developers to design and implement compensation logic that is matched to the business needs of each transaction.

With transaction compensation, the developer out of necessity takes an optimistic approach to transaction management. The assumption has to be made that the individual parts of the multisystem transaction will all be completed successfully. Many times that optimism is warranted. However, a loosely coupled transaction is not able to satisfy the ACID requirements of a distributed transaction as well as a transaction processing manager is. For example, isolation is problematic because multiple applications may each try to update the same data element within a very short time frame. Therefore, in the resort example, it is entirely possible for each of five travelers to believe that they have reserved the last rental car at the location that they are all visiting.

Also, if a transaction is cancelled before it's completed, it's not possible to have each system simply roll back those parts of the transaction that were successful. Instead, a compensating transaction must be run. For example, if the car is no longer available, a credit transaction has to be sent to the traveler's credit card company to compensate for the deposit that was just processed.

In addition to isolation, consistency is also compromised by transaction compensation. It's often easy to make changes to one system that are not immediately reflected in related systems.

---

**Note:** Standards associated with transaction compensation include WS-Transactions, WS-Orchestration, and BPEL4WS. For more information about these standards, see "Understanding Web Services Specifications," in the MSDN Web Services Developer Center (*http:// msdn.microsoft.com/webservices/understanding/specs/default.aspx*).

---

## Long-Running Transactions

Some business processes, particularly those that involve human interaction, run over an indefinite time period. Traditional management techniques are not useful for these types of transactions, because each transaction holds database locks and resources. Because thousands of business processes can run on a computer at any one time, the number of resources held rapidly becomes impractical.

To get around the problem, these business processes are treated as long-running transactions. Long-running transactions are specifically designed to group collections of actions into atomic units of work that can exist across time, organizations, and applications. A long-running transaction usually contains several nested short-running transactions, the overall grouping (composition) of which is controlled by the long-running transaction.

In a long-running distributed business process, records in a database cannot be locked for extended periods of time, nor can records be locked in databases distributed across organizations. This enables other transactions to see the data being used by the transaction.

A long-running transaction satisfies all of the conventional ACID requirements except isolation. However, where appropriate, a long-running transaction may consist of a series of short-lived transactions which do ensure isolation.

As an example, consider a business process that is initiated when a purchase order request is received. The request is logged to a database and is then sent to the request approver. It might take several days for the approval response to be received, at which point the response is also logged to a database and the purchase order is sent to the supplier. Receiving and logging both the initial request and the response are each composed of multiple actions (receiving and logging).

In this scenario, you can use short-lived transactions to group related actions into a single atomic transaction (receiving a message and logging it to the database). However, you cannot group the receipt of the purchase request message and the receipt of the approval message within a single short-lived transaction, because that would lock rows in the database for indefinite periods. Instead, you use a long-running transaction to group together the two short-lived transactions, which might be separated by a significant time period. Figure 2.6 illustrates this approach.

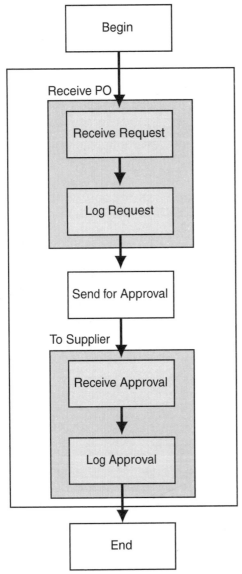

**Figure 2.6**
*Grouping short-lived transactions into a long-running transaction*

When the business process in Figure 2.6 is executed, the purchase request is received and the database is updated in a short-lived transaction. If anything goes wrong at this stage, the Receive PO transaction is aborted and no changes are made; otherwise, the transaction is committed. Then the schedule waits for the arrival of the approval message. When the message arrives, the database is again updated transactionally. However, if anything goes wrong at this stage, the To Supplier transaction will abort automatically. The Receive PO transaction cannot be aborted, though, because it has already been committed. In this event, the first transaction must supply a code that will perform transaction compensation.

### Timed Transactions

Timed transactions trigger an abort of a long-running transaction if it has not been completed in a specified amount of time. It is often very difficult to decide in advance how long a business process should take. However, it is possible to make a reasonable estimate of how long a specific action within a business process should take (for example, the arrival of a message).

A timed transaction can group short-lived transactions and wait for the arrival of a message within a specified time period. If the message arrives in time, the timed transaction is committed; otherwise, the timed transaction aborts and causes the short-lived transactions to execute compensation code.

# Summary

Effective application integration depends on having a good understanding of your environment. After you define the business requirements of your organization and understand how your applications resolve business problems, you can determine the characteristics and capabilities that your application integration environment requires. You must also understand the major challenges that are inherent in effective application integration and develop strategies to deal with those challenges.

# 3

# Security and Operational Considerations

As you consider the design of your application integration environment, it is very important to examine the security requirements of your organization. A well-designed application integration environment rapidly becomes an integral part of your organization. Therefore, security vulnerabilities in application integration have the potential to cause wide-ranging problems.

Similarly, your operational practices must be well-defined so that your application integration environment can continue to operate effectively and reliably over time. This chapter covers both the security and operations considerations you need to examine to ensure that your application integration environment continues to operate in a reliable and secure fashion.

## Security Considerations

Because different applications have different security requirements and features, it can be quite a challenge to ensure that your application integration environment functions properly without compromising your security requirements. Security is particularly important in application integration because a breach in an integration service may result in security breaches in other integrated systems.

### Security Policy

The first step toward effective security in any environment is creating a written security policy. Many factors can affect the security policy, including the value of the assets you are protecting, the threats that your environment faces, and the vulnerabilities that are currently present.

The security policy should form the basis of any security measures you take in your organization. Before you make modifications to the environment, you should ensure that they are consistent with your security policy. You should also examine the policy itself periodically to determine whether it needs to be redefined in the wake of new business requirements and to verify that the procedures and standards that implement the policy adhere to industry best practices.

> **Note:** This chapter examines only security policy that is related to integration technologies. Your policy, however, should cover all aspects of IT security, including physical security.

From an integration standpoint, your security policy should define:

- **A mechanism for evaluating and classifying threats**. Your evaluation mechanism should ensure that consistent and relevant information is gathered about any threat. This information helps you classify threats to ensure that high-level threats are not ignored and that low-level threats are not unnecessarily escalated.

- **A mechanism for acting on threats**. This should ensure that the appropriate people are involved in dealing with a threat and that they are equipped to deal with it in an appropriate manner.

- **A boundary for information security**. Most application integration environments include some form of integration with other organizations or individuals outside the boundary of your own IT environment. It is therefore very important to define the type of information that must be protected within the organization, between business partners, and from the public. You also must determine how that information should be protected in each of the different cases.

- **A plan for communication and enforcement**. One of the main problems in maintaining good security in an organization is ensuring that individuals are aware of the security policy. It is therefore vital that the security requirements (as defined in the policy) are clearly communicated to your employees, including both IT staff and the rest of the organization. You also need ways of ensuring that people comply with the requirements, including clearly defined disciplinary procedures where appropriate.

- **General security guidelines**. If you make the security guidelines in your security policy too specific, you run the risk of them quickly becoming obsolete. However, if they are too generic, you run the risk of making them too vague. Therefore, you need to maintain a delicate balance in defining an effective and lasting policy. Ensuring compliance to security guidelines across an entire enterprise can be problematic when different systems are being used. However, it is possible to provide some generic non-technology-specific guidelines that are unlikely to age too quickly. A good example of such a guideline is one that specifies a minimum level of encryption for public key/private key pairs in your environment. Of course, even a guideline such as this is likely to change as technology advances.

- **Reference to other documents**. Your policy should reference more specific security policy documents and an Incident Response Plan. Linking to other documents enables you to define more specific requirements that are likely to change frequently without having to modify the main security policy in your organization.

- **A mechanism for modifying security policies**. As your environment evolves and new threats and vulnerabilities emerge, you must modify your policies to make sure that they continue to reflect the requirements of your organization. Therefore, your security policy must define the mechanism for security policy change and must identify the people responsible for making changes.

## Security Capabilities

A number of basic capabilities are usually required to ensure effective security in an application integration environment. Table 3.1 shows these security capabilities.

**Table 3.1: Security Capabilities**

| Capability | Description |
|---|---|
| Authorization | Determines whether a particular connection attempt should be allowed. |
| Authentication | Verifies credentials when an application attempts to make a connection. |
| Information Protection | Prevents unauthorized users from easily viewing or tampering with information. |
| Identity Management | Manages multiple sets of credentials and maps them to the correct application. |
| Nonrepudiation | Uses digital signatures to verify identity. |
| Profile Management | Manages principal profiles. |
| Security Context Management | Determines how credentials are provided to applications. |

For more information about each of these capabilities, see the Appendix, "Application Integration Capabilities."

## Defining Your Security Requirements

The precise security requirements of your application integration environment depend on a number of factors, including the following:

- Security requirements of your organization
- Business requirements for application integration
- Technical requirements for application integration

- Capabilities of the applications you are integrating
- Platforms on which applications are running
- Budgetary constraints

As a starting point for defining your security requirements, you should perform a risk analysis. Doing so allows you to identify the threats and vulnerabilities that you face and identify the countermeasures you can deploy to keep risk at an appropriate level.

The following paragraphs discuss security requirements that are common to many application integration environments.

## Authentication

Multiple forms of authentication are available to you when integrating applications, and these forms provide varying levels of security. For example, HTTP Basic Authentication passes a user name and password back and forth in each request. The user name and password are not encrypted (just encoded), so capturing network traffic could potentially give an attacker easy access to the information.

HTTP Basic Authentication is not appropriate for most environments, although it can be used in some cases where the channel itself is secured (for example, when using Secure Sockets Layer, or SSL). However, because different operating systems implement different authentication protocols, one of the challenges of application integration is finding a secure form of authentication that is used on each of the platforms you need to support.

One common authentication protocol is Kerberos, because it is supported by both UNIX and the Microsoft® Windows® operating system (Windows 2000 and later). Kerberos is a network authentication protocol, defined by the Internet Engineering Task Force (IETF), that relies on public key cryptography. However, the use of Kerberos for authentication with third parties requires trust relationships to be established and access to the Kerberos key distribution center. The Kerberos key distribution center is where the private keys of *principals* (users or systems) are kept for encrypting information.

One way of increasing the security of authentication is to use multifactorial authentication. This form of authentication is increasingly used in situations where people interact with systems and is commonly referred to as *something you know, something you have, something you are*, defined as follows:

- Something you know—for example, a password or PIN number
- Something you have—for example, a smart card
- Something you are—for example, the unique patterns of your iris (the colored part of your eye)

Requiring two or more of these factors for authentication can dramatically increase the security of any environment. However, this form of authentication is not commonly used in system-to-system authentication.

In some cases, applications require authentication that is not integrated with the operating system. In such cases, you should investigate separately how authentication occurs (is the password sent over the network?) and how the password is stored at the target application (is it maintained in a plain text file?). In circumstances where the requesting application must present a password, you should also ensure that the requesting application stores the password securely.

One other important consideration is whether to use the same password across multiple applications. If you change the password in one location, how will that change be reflected in other locations? If you are using different passwords for each application, how can you ensure that the password information is kept current on each system? In complicated situations such as these, your application integration environment may need the Identity Management capability, which enables credentials for multiple applications to be associated with a single identity.

## Authorization

Two methods of authorization are most commonly used. One method is to perform authorization based on the user entity obtained through authentication. The other is to perform authorization based on user roles.

Authorization based on user identities is becoming less common in many systems and applications available today because it is more cumbersome to manage, particularly in large-scale implementations. In many cases, when a user changes a job role, or begins work on a new project, he or she requires access to an entirely new group of systems. You may need to do a lot of administrative work to give the user permissions that correspond to the new job role.

Role-based authorization works around this problem by allowing you to decouple user identities from the roles the users assume and resources or services they can access. A role is a category or set of users who share the same security privileges. For example, imagine that today Jane is a credit manager who is allowed to view customer credit details, but next month Jane will be transferring to another department as a human resources manager. With role-based authorization, the credit manager role will still be allowed to access the resource, but Jane will not be able to access the resource when she commences her new role.

From an application integration perspective, authorization can occur at three different levels:

- **System**. System-level authorization is the more commonly used type of authorization, where the system protects resources. A typical example of resources is files stored in the file system that are protected by the operating system. System-level authorization is also commonly used for network shares.

- **Functional**. Functional-level authorization protects resources based on functional ability, which usually ties authorization to specific applications or services. For example, an integration application may expose two services named GetCustomerDetailsInternal and GetCustomerDetailsExternal. The former service can only be called by systems located within the organization (internal systems). The latter can be called by internal systems as well as external systems (possibly from a business partner).

- **Data**. Data-level authorization provides the lowest granular level of authorization. This capability is usually tied very closely to the business logic of the service. The integration application from the previous example may merge the GetCustomerDetails services into a single smarter service. When internal systems call the resulting service, it provides additional data that it excludes when external systems call the service.

In many cases, these different types of authorization are implemented using different technologies and are located in different layers of the systems. For example, the system-level authorization may be performed and maintained by the operating system; the functional authorization level may be performed and maintained by an integration product; and the data authorization may be custom-coded, because it is usually very closely linked with the business logic and requires detailed knowledge of the data to be protected. However, even though the three types of authorization levels may be implemented in different layers of the systems, all of the principals and access control information may be placed within a single security directory.

## Security Tokens

Often systems issue unique tokens or tickets after authentication and authorization has been performed. The idea behind token-based security is to allow the system to quickly recognize and trust the requester, which reduces the authentication and authorization overhead. There are a number of different ways to implement tokens, but most of the standard authentication protocols provide token-based security after the initial authentication and authorization. Token-based mechanisms have the advantage that the actual requester's credentials are not always passed around the network.

When you use security tokens, reply attacks can be a problem. These attacks involve the use of specialized software that is able to capture network data packets. The captured packets are then modified and replayed. To protect against reply attacks, you can use rolling tokens, which are changed or renewed within a short interval of time. Limiting the time available to capture, modify, and replay packets greatly reduces the chance of network capture and replay. Kerberos specifically addresses the prevention of replay attacks.

## Security Context Management

When implementing security context management, you need to determine whether to use impersonation, consolidation, or both. Impersonation is not commonly implemented in application integration scenarios because of problems with maintaining user identities across the different applications being integrated. In such scenarios, a matching user identity must be present in each of the systems. However, with the increasing availability and capability of identity management systems, this requirement may change. Using exact user credentials to access the various systems provides better ability to track the service requester's request from various systems and allows authorization to occur at the systems that need to implement it. Figure 3.1 shows impersonation using an identity management system.

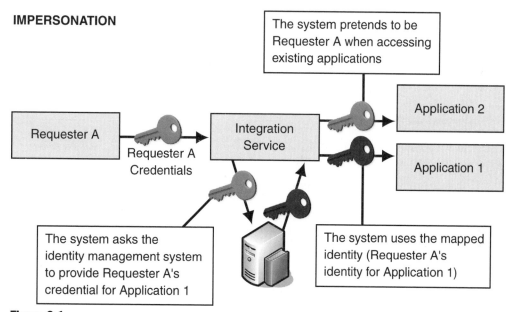

**IMPERSONATION**

The system pretends to be Requester A when accessing existing applications

Requester A

Requester A Credentials

Integration Service

Application 2

Application 1

The system asks the identity management system to provide Requester A's credential for Application 1

The system uses the mapped identity (Requester A's identity for Application 1)

**Figure 3.1**

*Using impersonation for security context management*

If you use consolidation for security context management, a single identity is used to identify the requester to each application. This allows all requesters to have the same level of authority. Composed applications commonly use consolidation because it provides simple user management to the existing systems and a better opportunity for connection pooling capabilities. Figure 3.2 on the next page shows consolidation being used.

**CONSOLIDATION**

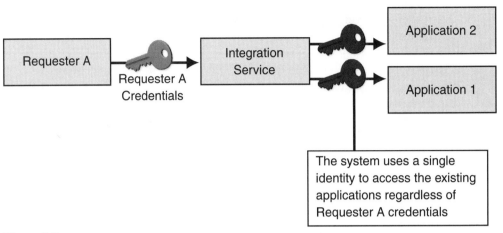

**Figure 3.2**
*Using consolidation for security context management*

## Information Protection

You must determine when it is appropriate to use encryption, hashing, and obfuscation in your application integration environment, and how to implement them.

Encryption is often used in an application integration environment to protect application data as it passes across the network. It may also be used to protect user names and passwords if they have to be passed as plain text.

The two main implementation choices for encryption are secret key encryption and public key encryption. One of the biggest issues with secret key encryption is the requirement for the sender and recipient of the data to have the same secret key. The more parties involved in the communication chain, the more places the secret key has to be distributed and the greater the risk of jeopardizing the key. The encrypted data is usually tied to the exact key used to encrypt the information. If the key is changed, existing encrypted data must be decrypted and reencrypted with the new key. For this reason, public key encryption is often a better choice; however, if you do not currently have a public key infrastructure, you must implement one to support public key encryption.

## Web Services Security

As Web services become an increasingly common communication protocol for application integration, it is likely that the Web Services Security (WS-Security) specification and related extension specifications will emerge as the industry-accepted security communication protocol.

WS-Security provides a higher-level protocol but does not provide the ability to perform authentication, it merely provides a common language for a variety of systems on different platforms. You will need to consider the best mechanism for securing the service while ensuring that the target audiences can participate with minimal or no interoperability issues. For now, you may still need to rely on the combination of SSL, user name and password, and tokens to authenticate Web service requests when using HTTP as the transport mechanism.

# Operational Management Considerations

Even after you build an application integration environment and it is running successfully, your work does not stop there. The environment will need to be monitored and maintained over time. This section discusses the various operational management considerations involved. Implementing the capabilities listed in this section should help to ensure that your architecture continues to function as smoothly as possible.

Operational management is a large topic that covers a broad range of technical and process-oriented issues. Many books, software, and Web resources discuss the various aspects of operational management. In this guide, the discussion is restricted to technically oriented aspects of operational management, specifically to those that are relevant to application integration.

**Note:** This guide does not discuss processes-oriented considerations; however, effective operations require technology to provide system information, correct interpretation of the information, and processes to ensure adherence to an overall plan. Deficiency in any of these areas leads to poor operational management.

## Defining an Operational Management Policy

As with security, an important part of effective operations is to have a predefined operational management policy, which defines how operations occur throughout your organization. If you currently have a policy for operational management, you should make sure that your application integration environment meets the requirements specified there. If you do not have such a policy, designing your application integration environment represents an excellent opportunity to institute a more organized approach to operations.

Your operational management policy, at the minimum, should provide the following information:

- Clearly defined terminologies and target metrics
- Methodology and/or formulas for measuring the metrics to ensure that results are consistent
- Service-level prioritization to ensure that the most important policies are followed first

You should make sure that any policy and service-level metrics clearly define terminology. For example, if you simply state that a system needs to be available 99.999 percent of the time, you often find that you are not defining your requirements appropriately. When you examine the situation in more detail, you often find that the business unit only requires very high availability within business operations hours.

## Operational Management Services

A number of basic capabilities are usually required to ensure effective operational management in an application integration environment. Table 3.2 shows these capabilities.

**Table 3.2: Operational Management Capabilities**

| Capability | Description |
| --- | --- |
| Business Activity Management | Monitors, manages, and analyzes business transactions processed by the integration system. |
| Event Handling | Receives events and acts on them. |
| Configuration Management | Tracks hardware and software configuration. |
| Directory | Maintains information on applications, subscriptions, and services. |
| Change Management | Manages change within the application integration environment. |
| System Monitoring | Determines whether the hardware, operating system, and software applications are functioning as expected, and within the desired operating parameters or agreed-upon service levels. |

For more information about each of these capabilities, see Appendix A, "Application Integration Capabilities."

## Defining Your Operational Management Requirements

As with security requirements, the precise operational management requirements of your application integration environment depend on a number of factors, including the following:

- The operational management requirements of your organization
- The business requirements for application integration
- The technical requirements for application integration
- The capabilities of the applications you are integrating
- The platforms on which applications are running
- Budgetary constraints

The following paragraphs discuss operational management considerations that are common to many application integration environments.

## System Monitoring

Your application integration environment typically involves multiple applications running on multiple computer systems. To keep your environment running successfully, you must monitor the system to ensure that each element of the application integration environment is functioning properly and is meeting its performance goals.

One challenging aspect of system monitoring in an application integration environment is that information often is spread across multiple systems in different geographic locations. It is therefore particularly useful to have a system that can aggregate the performance data in one centralized location where it can be analyzed. Because data aggregation is one of the goals of application integration itself, you can often use the data capabilities of your application integration environment to support your System Monitoring capability.

Your system monitoring should focus on the following areas:

- **System and application health**. Tracking the health status of the system and the application. A healthy system or application can perform its operations within expected parameters or agreed service levels.

- **System and application performance monitoring**. Tracking the system and application response times for service requests.

- **Security monitoring**. Monitoring security related events and audit trails.

- **Service-level monitoring**. Monitoring the system and application adherence to agreed or predefined service levels.

The following paragraphs discuss each type of system monitoring in more detail.

### System and Application Health Monitoring

In an application integration environment, you need to ensure that the operating system, the applications, and the capabilities that facilitate application integration are all functioning properly. In some cases, you may need to design a special module within the integration logic to perform basic diagnostics of all the components it uses, or create a special test case using specific data (called from a probe) that returns a well-known result if the system is functioning properly.

In some cases, your applications may be instrumented and therefore may provide useful information about their health. However, in situations where an application is not generating that data, either because it is not configured to, or because it is unable to, you can get further information by issuing a probing test from an external system or another application within the system. By using regular probes, you can detect unavailable systems and raise an alert. Setting very frequent probes may affect system or application performance, but setting infrequent probes means that you will be unable to quickly detect unavailable systems. The interval for probes you set should be based on the maximum desired elapse time. For example, if you set probes to occur 10 minutes apart, in the worst-case scenario the alert will not be generated until 10 minutes after the system becomes available.

Often system health is thought of simply in terms of whether the system is up or down. In reality, however, health is not just a binary value. Just as human health is not just measured according to whether the person is dead or alive, a computer can be unhealthy and yet still function, albeit at reduced capacity.

For example, if your application is designed and tested to handle 100 concurrent users and respond within 2 seconds for requests, you can consider it healthy if it meets this criterion. If it takes 30 seconds to respond to requests, you will probably consider it to be unhealthy.

By detecting and diagnosing unhealthy applications early, you can prevent a system or application outage. There are numerous possibilities for systems to become unhealthy during operations, including:

- **Virus or malicious attack**. A virus usually consumes system resources or alters system behavior. The impact of viruses can range from having no noticeable effect to rendering the system useless. Malicious attacks come in two forms: internal intrusion and external attacks. Internal intrusion is when the attacker tries to gain control and penetrate the system. This form of attack is usually difficult to detect because the attacker intends to be discreet. A problem may not be apparent from a system and application health perspective, even though a security breach has occurred. External attacks usually come in the form of denial of service (DoS). The main purpose of these attacks is to prevent the system from providing services. A system that is hit by a DoS attack can be considered as sick or dead, depending on whether it is still able to process requests. Installing antivirus software and ensuring that it is updated is a good start to battling viruses. However, you should also monitor system requests and probe your applications to ensure that your service levels are being met. If they are not, this is a potential indication that you are undergoing some form of malicious attack.

- **Unplanned increase in usage**. A sudden and unforeseen increase in usage gener- ally affects externally facing systems that provide services to anonymous service requesters. Such usage increases can render a system sick, because it was never designed to handle the increased load and maintain the agreed-upon service level. If you provide artificial limits or queuing, you can allow additional loads to be handled in a predictable manner. Systems that create new threads to handle requests can be very susceptible to spikes (or storms). If the spikes are large enough to cause the system to generate enormous amounts of threads, it can overload the operating system so that it becomes too busy to manage the threads and cannot allocate resources to handle the actual requests.

- **Failure in resilient systems**. To provide fault tolerance in your environment, you may use resilient systems, such as Web farms. If one of the servers fails in this type of environment, the system can still function at reduced capacity. It is extremely important that you detect failed servers and fix them as soon as possible so that the system can return to full capacity. You should make sure that you know exactly how many types and levels of failure your resilient systems can handle before the system itself will fail. The majority of Web farms implemented today use pin-level packets, which means an application can be unavailable and still receive requests. In these cases, failures can be very difficult to detect because the service to the end user does not always suffer in a predictable manner.

Integration applications generally rely quite heavily on message-based communications. This type of asynchronous communication provides good scalability, but it can also make it difficult for you to detect failures in communication paths. Most message-based products use dead letter queues to inform the application if any messages fail to arrive or fail to be consumed by the receiving system.

### System and Application Performance Monitoring

You should use performance monitoring to ensure that application integration is adhering to agreed-upon or predefined service levels. Performance monitoring also gives you an early indication of potential failures or future capacity issues. The two main areas important to integration application for performance monitoring are:

- System response time measurements
- Resource usage measurements

By measuring system responses for all aspects of a request, you can help to ensure early detection of potential bottlenecks. It is fairly easy to measure performance at a general level, such as the average number of requests per second and the average amount of time it took to process a request. However, one of the more useful items you can track through performance monitoring is delayed responses to requests as they go through the system. Doing so allows you to determine if a delay was the result of a particular request type or other factors. For example, for a purchase order handling system that relies on a number of back-end systems, a particular purchase order that calls back-end system A with more than 100 items may result in an unusually slow response from that system. Without adequate monitoring and tracking, you would find it very difficult to trace the problems based on pattern analysis.

Resource usage measurements help you to determine whether your systems have adequate resources to run at their full potential. Inadequate resources can lead to resource contention, where the lack of resources causes degradation to system performance. If you keep historical information on resource usage, you can track and predict increases in resource usage.

You can also use longer-term observations of performance and resource usage tracking to establish useable baselines. This technique is particularly useful if you need to increase performance or reduce resource usage.

### Security Monitoring

Your application integration environment generally requires secure communications between applications within your organization. As mentioned earlier in this chapter, security is vital in all integration application design. However, the security of your systems depends not only on the design and implementation of the software, but also on appropriate monitoring or auditing capabilities. As an example, imagine that an operating system does not provide the ability to track failed logons. It is very difficult to check if someone is trying to attack a particular account, because system operators have no way of detecting such attacks.

At the minimum, your security monitoring should provide the following capabilities:

- **Logon audit log**. For tracking logon information. You may want to track all logons, but you should certainly track all unsuccessful logons. The integrity of the security audit log is paramount. The log content should be kept secured with the data available only in read-only mode and accessible to the minimum number of people.

- **Data access log**. For tracking all access to the data repository. This capability is very important if the original requester identity is used to access the data. As mentioned earlier in this chapter, some systems provide the ability to perform single sign-on or impersonation. The value of the data access log diminishes if the system consolidates the various requester identities into a single identity used to access the data.

- **Security policy modification log**. For tracking all changes made to the security policy. This capability is important in detecting changes that relax the security policy, including changes due to human error and changes by hackers or disgruntled operators.

- **Alert mechanism**. An active alerting mechanism is needed to flag suspicious or unusual occurrences. Simply relying on logging is not adequate because the system can generate a large volume of log information. You should provide a rule-based alerting mechanism that allows critical or important analysis to be done automatically.

One very important part of security monitoring is ensuring that the security logs themselves are secure. You must ensure that security logs are accessible only to authorized personnel and that the information captured cannot be modified. Solutions for protecting the log information can involve storing the information on a read-only device and also providing signatures, as a secondary measure, to allow verification of information integrity.

## Business Activity Management

Business Activity Management provides probably the greatest potential to clearly demonstrate return on investment to the business owners. Nonetheless, it is one of the areas often left out in integration environments. The short development time for many IT projects often causes the monitoring aspects of a system to be designed last or never designed at all, because they are viewed as an additional benefit. To provide efficient and valuable Business Activity Management capabilities, you should ensure that the correct information is captured during design and development.

To provide you with added value in the longer term, your Business Activity Management should at the minimum provide the following capabilities:

- **Business transaction exception handling**. This capability allows you to handle transactions that generate business-level exceptions. For example, your system has paused the processing of a loan approval because the credit rating of the applicant was borderline. However, after checking manually, your loan officer has decided to approve the loan. Rather than rejecting the applications and forcing the applications to start from the beginning, your system should provide the capability for the loan officer to reroute the transaction.

- **Contextual monitoring**. You should be able to track the progress of any business transaction through the process chain. Providing response times at each level of the business step (whether it was processed by a system or by a person) allows you to determine any cause of delays in the process.

- **Rules-based alerting**. This capability allows you to generate alerts due to business events. This means that you can detect anomalies and potential delays in processing. Early detection of potential delays gives you the opportunity to contact the party that originated the transaction and inform them of the problem in advance, or to fix the problem before it affects them.

- **Historical data mining**. This capability allows you to capture useful business process information, such as the time it took to process each process step, the data sources for the business process, and the next step in the process. You can analyze the information and then modify your business processes if needed. Generally, the more information you can capture the better, because having more information means that there are more ways to take apart and analyze the data. It is also helpful because you cannot be sure now what information will be useful in the future.

## Event Handling

In an application integration environment, if one application raises an event, it often leads to actions in other applications. An unexpected event or exception in one application may lead to the failure of another application, for example. To ensure that your application integration environment is stable, you should have the capabilities to receive system events from your applications and take actions to ensure that other applications and systems react appropriately to maintain service.

In many cases, an exception at the system level leads to particular failures at the business process level. You should therefore have capabilities for dealing with events at the business process level as well. However, it is often useful for the events at the system level to be passed up to the business process level, because a system event may well be the first indication of a potential failure at the business process level.

### Change and Configuration Management

Application integration environments are notoriously difficult to manage, because they tend to involve increasing numbers of applications communicating on multiple disparate systems. You should therefore consider the benefits that good change and configuration management bring to your application integration environment.

Implementing change and configuration management effectively is a major project in itself, which can generate significant initial costs. Fortunately, however, you will complete some of the significant work required for effective change and configuration management as you define your application integration environment—for example, developing an understanding of how applications communicate with each other and which systems they run on. If you can define the requirements of your change and configuration management system prior to your work on defining your application integration requirements, you can significantly reduce the costs of implementing change and configuration management.

### Directory

Your application integration environment may contain multiple directories that contain information about identities, profiles, subscriptions (used in a publish/subscribe scenario), application configuration, and capabilities. Alternatively, this information may all be located in separate parts of a single directory. As you define your application integration environment, you should determine which of this information you need to store and where you will store it.

Most modern operating systems are based on an extensible directory that can be used to store the information required by application integration. Such a directory can be particularly useful in situations where your organization uses one operating system. However, in cases where multiple operating systems are used, it is possible to synchronize each directory into a meta-directory. Alternatively, you may want to store your directory information separate from the operating system and use the capabilities of your application integration environment itself to facilitate replication.

# Summary

An application integration environment cannot function successfully if you do not carefully consider the security and operations requirements you face. These considerations are particularly important because application integration issues are likely to span many departments within your organization. As you define your application environment, you should use the opportunity to look again at the security and operations practices within your organization and to determine whether they should be modified. If you consider security and operations practices early and give them sufficient emphasis, you will increase the chance of your application integration environment operating securely and reliably over time.

# 4

# Using Microsoft Technologies for Application Integration

Now that you have examined the requirements for an application integration environment, it is useful to examine some of the products that will help you address your application integration needs. This chapter discusses the Microsoft® technologies that you can use to achieve effective application integration, and how they map to the capabilities described in this guide.

## Microsoft Technologies Used for Application Integration

Microsoft provides many products that you can apply to solve application integration problems, including BizTalk® Server, SQL Server™, Host Integration Server (HIS), and Microsoft Operations Manager (MOM). In addition, Microsoft delivers numerous technologies as part of the Microsoft Windows Server™ operating system, including Internet Information Services (IIS), the Active Directory® directory service, Message Queuing (also known as MSMQ), the Microsoft .NET Framework, and various XML technologies.

BizTalk Server 2004 is the main server product used to address application integration. BizTalk Server delivers specific integration technologies, such as mapping and orchestration, and in addition uses many of the underlying services provided by the operating system, SQL Server, and Microsoft Windows® SharePoint™ Services.

You can also use numerous other Microsoft technologies individually to solve application integration problems, including SQL Server, HIS, MOM, and the many services and features of the Windows Server 2003 operating system itself.

The remainder of this chapter introduces each of these Microsoft technologies and products, shows when you might consider using them, and details the tradeoffs that you should consider when using them.

# BizTalk Server 2004

BizTalk Server enables you to define business processes that connect systems, people, and trading partners through manageable business processes. BizTalk Server builds on the Windows Server operating system and the .NET Framework.

You can use the following BizTalk Server features as part of your application integration environment:

- **Automation of business processes** allows you to reduce human involvement in certain parts of your environment.

- **Business Activity Monitoring** (BAM) gives information workers a real-time view of running business processes with Microsoft Office tools such as Microsoft Excel.

- **Real-time tracking** enables you to follow the real-time progress of documents and processes in your BizTalk Server applications.

- **Integration with the Microsoft Visual Studio® .NET development system** increases developer productivity through a common development environment, and inheriting all the capabilities of Visual Studio .NET and the .NET Framework.

- **Integration with the Microsoft Office InfoPath™ information gathering program** enhances information worker productivity by making the most of tools they already know how to use (specifically, applications in the Office suite). InfoPath is a Microsoft Office System program that provides an information worker–friendly front end to BizTalk Server 2004 for entering XML and consuming Web services.

- **Single sign-on** provides unified authentication between heterogeneous systems and applications (both those based on Windows and those that are not based on Windows).

- **Human-based workflow** integrates people and processes with a single orchestration engine.

- **Support for Business Process Execution Language (BPEL)** simplifies cross-platform interoperability for process orchestration with standards developed in conjunction with other industry leaders.

- **Support for Web services** provides ground-up support for Web services standards such as Web Services Description Language (WSDL) and Universal Description, Discovery, and Integration (UDDI). Referencing and building Web services for orchestration is a simple process in the integrated development environment.

- **Business rules** enable you to dynamically change business processes to maximize organizational flexibility.

# Host Integration Server 2000

Host Integration Server 2000 enables users running Windows operating systems to share resources on mainframes and AS/400 systems without requiring system administrators to install resource-heavy Systems Network Architecture (SNA) protocols on their computers or to install specialized software on the host computers.

HIS provides data integration components, which provide desktop or server-based applications with direct access to host data, including relational and nonrelational mainframe data and AS/400 data, through open database connectivity (ODBC), OLE DB, and Component Object Model (COM) automation controls.

HIS is typically used in application integration to provide components that allow Web-based or Windows-based applications to communicate directly with host-based systems. For example, a BizTalk Server–based application integration solution can use HIS to Web-enable a host-based application. In addition, HIS also provides a bridging technology between IBM's MQ Series messaging system and Microsoft Message Queuing.

SQL Server often forms an integral part of an application integration environment, providing databases that you need to integrate, but also providing services that you can use directly in application integration. Two of the most important services are Data Transformation Services (DTS) and SQL Server Analysis Services.

## Data Transformation Services

Data Transformation Services (DTS) is a group of services delivered by SQL Server 2000 that provide the ability to automate routines that extract, transform, and load data from heterogeneous sources. DTS can extract, transform, and load heterogeneous data using OLE DB, ODBC, or text-only files into any supported OLE DB database or multidimensional store. DTS also automates data transformation by allowing the user to import or transform data automatically on a regularly scheduled basis.

You can access and manipulate DTS operations through interfaces that allow their programs to interact at multiple points during the progression of data transformations. DTS packages can be saved as code in the Visual Basic development system. DTS provides high-throughput parsing and data transformation that is suitable for specific point-to-point integration requirements.

## Analysis Services

SQL Server 2000 Analysis Services is a middle-tier service for online analytical processing (OLAP) and data mining. The Analysis Services system includes a server that manages multidimensional cubes of data for analysis and provides client access to cube information. Analysis Services organizes data from a data warehouse into cubes with precalculated aggregation data to provide fast answers to complex analytical queries. Analysis Services also enables you to create data-mining models from both multidimensional and relational data sources.

OLAP can be used in combination with the PivotTable Service and Excel (or applications from other vendors) to retrieve and present data about the integration application. BizTalk Server uses Analysis Services in exactly this way, providing both administrative- and business activity–focused reporting.

# Windows Server 2003

Windows Server 2003 provides operating system services, Web services, and the.NET Framework programming model. Together, these provide an ideal environment for the development of application integration solutions.

Windows Server 2003 can assume various roles in a network environment, including the File and Print role and the Application Server role. Key application integration services provided by Windows Server 2003 include Active Directory, IIS, and Message Queuing.

## Active Directory

In addition to providing directory services to the operating system itself, Active Directory also provides APIs that give access to the data stored in a directory for use by custom applications. For example, you can use Active Directory Service Interfaces (ADSI) to manage application resources from within the directory service. Microsoft products such as BizTalk Server typically use Active Directory for authentication and role-based access control.

With ADSI, you can use high-level development tools such as Visual Basic, Microsoft Visual C#®, or Microsoft Visual C++® to create directory-enabled applications. ADSI can also be used to access other directory services by accessing each one through its own provider. This means ADSI can be used to integrate multiple directories across disparate platforms, such as Lightweight Directory Access Protocol (LDAP), Novell Directory Services (NDS), or the Microsoft Windows NT® version 4.0 Security Account Manager (SAM).

## Internet Information Services

The Windows operating system uses IIS to receive HTTP and SOAP requests, and deliver HTTP and SOAP responses to external applications. IIS also serves as a platform for delivering application integration solutions deployed as Web services.

### Message Queuing and MSMQT

Microsoft Message Queuing (also known as MSMQ) is a Microsoft implementation of a reliable messaging system. Message Queuing comes with most Microsoft operating systems. Message Queuing provides both a reliable transport (a specific format of message transmission, over a specific TCP port) and physical queues on the server, managed by a queue manager.

Message Queuing supports interoperability with other messaging systems, most notably IBM's MQ Series. These other systems, referred to as foreign messaging systems, can be other Message Queuing systems or non-Message Queuing systems.

BizTalk Server 2004 uses a new technology called BizTalk Message Queuing (MSMQT). MSMQT uses the Message Queuing transport (the same protocol, over the same port), so it interoperates transparently with Message Queuing systems (and thus also with MQ Series systems by using connectivity toolkits).

## XML Technologies

Microsoft provides full support for XML technologies and has also defined some additional enhancements to XML that can be used with Microsoft technologies.

### XML Parser

From a developer's point of view, XML parsers are the fundamental XML component because they act as a bridge between XML documents, seen as a long chain of bytes, and applications that process the XML. Almost all XML applications are built on top of parsers. On Microsoft operating systems, the XML Document Object Model (DOM) is deployed both as a COM component and as managed components.

The parser is responsible for handling XML syntax and, optionally, checking the contents of the document against constraints established in a document type definition (DTD) or schema; the application must understand how to process or display the information. The application is insulated from the details of the XML document, allowing document creators to take advantage of those details without concerning themselves with the application.

### XSLT

By combining XML data with an XSLT transformation style sheet, you can dynamically transform data from one representation to another, and provide a presentation format for the information. XSLT style sheets are similar to cascading style sheets; however, they allow you not only to present XML data, but also to transform it into new data that is tailored specifically to a particular user, media, or client. With XSLT, you can transform data into device-aware or customer-aware information. BizTalk Server uses this technology to convert inbound documents into outbound documents by using XSLT "maps."

## Web Services

A Web service is a programmable entity that gives you a particular element of functionality, such as application logic, and is accessible to any number of potentially disparate systems that use Internet standards such as XML and HTTP. Web services depend heavily on the broad acceptance of XML and other Internet standards to create an infrastructure that supports application interoperability at a level that solves many of the problems that previously hindered such attempts.

A Web service can be used internally by a single application or exposed externally over the Internet for use by a number of applications. Because it is accessible through a standard interface, a Web service allows heterogeneous systems to work together as a single web of computation.

Web services use XML-based messaging as a fundamental means of data communication to help bridge differences between systems that use incongruent component models, operating systems, and programming languages. You can create applications that weave together Web services from a variety of sources in much the same way that you traditionally use components when creating a distributed application.

In the .NET Framework, Web service support is provided by the common language runtime. Many client and server Microsoft applications also either consume or provide Web service interfaces. For example, Microsoft InfoPath 2003 provides a rich-client interface that can use Web services to interoperate with BizTalk Server. BizTalk Server itself is able both to consume existing Web services and to expose business processes as new Web services.

## Web Services Enhancements

The basic Web service specification does not resolve many architectural problems such as how to route messages, ensure reliable delivery, or coordinate distributed work using compensating transactions. To address these issues, a collection of Web service architecture protocols have been written by Microsoft, IBM, and others that provide additional functionality. Web Services Enhancements (WSE) is one implementation of (or a subset of) these protocols.

Web Services Enhancements version 1.0 for Microsoft .NET is a new library for building Web services using the latest Web services protocols. This version focuses on the basic message-level protocols: WS-Security, WS-Routing (and WS-Referral), and Direct Internet Message Encapsulation (DIME) and WS-Attachments. WSE integrates with ASP.NET Web services, offering a simple way to extend their functionality. BizTalk Server can use these enhancements by adding custom components in the BizTalk Server pipelines to implement WSE security, for example.

## Windows SharePoint Services

Windows SharePoint Services enables you to create Web sites for information sharing and document collaboration. SharePoint sites are made up of Web Parts and ASP.NET–based components. Web Parts are designed to be added to pages and configured by site administrators and users, creating complete page-based applications.

Windows SharePoint Services sites extend file storage, providing communities for team collaboration and making it easy for users to work together on documents, tasks, contacts, events, and other information. Microsoft BizTalk Server uses this infrastructure to enable you to publish the results of Business Activity Monitoring on a Windows SharePoint Services site.

## Microsoft Operations Manager

Microsoft Operations Manager 2000 (MOM) is a network monitoring solution that captures and reports events throughout your network. By defining rules, you can automate responses or assign problems to a specific staff member for resolution. MOM displays information about service-level exceptions, open alerts, and computers in the configuration. You can check specific alert and event details, performance data, and monitored computer status.

MOM provides proactive real-time system monitoring for servers and computers throughout the enterprise that are running Windows 2000 and Windows 2003. MOM also displays useful information about computers and their alerts. You can display a view of all computers to see computer properties, alerts, events, performance, computer group membership, and the processing rules applied to each computer in the configuration group.

In addition to monitoring specific aspects of Windows Server operating systems, MOM can also load management packs, which allow it to be extended to monitor various Microsoft server applications.

# Mapping Microsoft Technologies to Application Integration Capabilities

To determine which Microsoft technologies you should use in your application integration environment, it is important to understand how the available technologies map to the capabilities defined in this guide. The capabilities are defined as follows:

- Business process integration capabilities
- Data integration capabilities
- Communications capabilities
- Security capabilities
- Operational management capabilities

## Business Process Integration Capabilities Provided by Microsoft Technologies

This guide defines a number of capabilities that are required for effective business process integration. Table 4.1 shows how Microsoft technologies provide these business process integration capabilities.

**Table 4.1: Business Process Integration Capabilities Provided by Microsoft Technologies**

| Capability | Provided by |
|---|---|
| Rules Processing | Custom .NET Framework components, SQL Server stored procedures, and BizTalk Server Business Rules Engine |
| Transaction Management and Compensation | Microsoft Distributed Transaction Coordinator (DTC) and BizTalk Server long-running transactions |
| Workflow | BizTalk Server Human Workflow Services |
| Orchestration | BizTalk Orchestration service |
| State Management | Common language runtime, IIS session management, and BizTalk Server orchestration state management |
| Event Processing | SQL Server triggers, MSMQ Events, and BizTalk Server messaging subscriptions |
| Schedule | Windows Server Schedule service and SQL Server Job Scheduler |
| Contract Management | BizTalk Orchestration service (BPEL4WS) |

It is useful to look at these capabilities in more detail.

## Rules Processing

When you need to implement new business rules as part of your application integration solution, the business rules vary widely in complexity and in how they are implemented. In typical business applications, you can develop business rules using SQL Server stored procedures or .NET Framework components. In BizTalk Server–based solutions, low-level business rules are often implemented in the messaging pipelines (validation rules, generally), in the data manipulation functions (data conversion rules, generally), or in the orchestration system (business rules implemented as .NET Framework components, for example).

All of these mechanisms have a significant disadvantage: Changes to the business rules require a recompile and redeployment of the appropriate component(s) that implement the business rule. Another disadvantage of these methods of implementing business rules is that the rules are expressed in terms of implementation artifacts (such as a specific field in an XML schema), rather than in a vocabulary based on the business process itself.

To assist with these issues, BizTalk Server provides a Business Rules Engine through which you design, build, compose, and manage your unique business rules. Business rules are statements that govern the conduct of business processes. The Business Rules Framework enables you to independently and seamlessly change code, processes, and rules by updating rules and the policies that contain them without having to update code as you would in a traditional development cycle.

## Transaction Management and Compensation

XA-compliant transactions or Atomicity, Consistency, Isolation, Durability (ACID) transactions are implemented using a two-phase commit protocol and are managed in a Microsoft environment by the DTC. BizTalk Server supports XA-compliant transactions through the DTC. The DTC is used when performing synchronous database updates or when accessing other transactional resources. It also provides support for long-running transactions and timed transactions.

All of the transaction types supported by BizTalk Server provide the ability to specify compensation logic, which allows the results of transactions to be undone or provides an alternate series of actions to take if a transaction is aborted. Compensation logic is necessary even for short-lived transactions, because some of the actions performed within the context of the short-lived transaction may not themselves be transactional. By using compensation logic for failure processing, you can add additional error handling semantics to schedules for all transaction types.

## Human Workflow Services

Human Workflow Services (HWS) uses the BizTalk Server orchestration engine and interfaces with Microsoft Office products. HWS provides a workflow model that involves human interaction rather than fully automated business processes. It allows business activities to be captured as a workflow, and is designed to be modular enough to be used as a stand-alone component or as part of a larger business process. Workflows in HWS are created by composing a series of tasks, or *actions*, such as Delegate, Approve, Review, and Escalate, which are associated with users based on their roles.

## Orchestration

BizTalk Orchestration provides a rich programming environment, which includes a visual design and development environment that you can use to separate the business process being developed from the implementation of that process. The environment supports a complete set of programming constructs, including transactions and exception processing semantics, support for long-running processes, and state management.

A BizTalk orchestration is an application running within the .NET Framework managed environment. The application itself uses a graphical programming language with its own specific semantics, which is then compiled to Microsoft intermediate language (MSIL). The graphical programming language has many of the same constructs and rules as a C# application, along with custom constructs designed to suit long-running business applications.

You can specify an implementation for each of the individual actions that make up a business process and compile this information into an executable representation. These business processes are physical processes, which are initiated by some event (such as the arrival of a message) and then may run for an extended duration (weeks or months), sending messages to, and receiving messages from, other systems in the enterprise, or from parties external to the enterprise.

## State Management

Microsoft products handle state in a variety of ways. Of particular note in application integration solutions is the way in which state is handled in a Web-based integration solution (in ASP.NET), and how state is handled in a .NET Framework application.

ASP.NET provides the following application-state support:

- A state facility that is compatible with earlier versions of ASP.
- An application-state dictionary that is available to all request handlers invoked within an application.
- A synchronization mechanism that enables you to coordinate concurrent access to variables stored in the application state.
- Application-state values that are accessible only from code running within the context of the originating application.

Because a BizTalk orchestration is actually a .NET Framework application, state is automatically managed within each instance of an orchestration, meaning that state information is maintained both within the messages flowing through the orchestration and in local or global variables declared within the orchestration.

BizTalk Orchestration also provides the ability to back up the entire state of an orchestration instance to the database and, when necessary, to restore the orchestration instance with all state information. This mechanism is referred to as dehydration/rehydration and is required to support the deployment of huge numbers of orchestration instances running over an extended period of time.

## Event Processing

The message transports available in Windows all provide some form of event trigger on the arrival of a message, which allows applications to react to this event. Message Queuing provides triggers, which bind Message Queuing message arrival to a COM object or to the instantiation of a process. Similarly, SQL Server provides data triggers, which are fired as the result of some data update.

Within a BizTalk orchestration, the arrival of a new message also acts as an application event. A new message arriving at the system will either instantiate a new instance of the business process (instantiate a new orchestration instance), or the message will correlate with an existing instance of a business process. For example, a purchase order acknowledgment will correlate with the instance of the business process to which it corresponds. An event may also be initiated by a .NET Framework component. This mechanism may be used to synchronize the orchestration with external events.

## Schedule

Microsoft products provide various scheduling services. The Schedule service in Windows Server handles application-level scheduling. In SQL Server, SQL jobs are scheduled with a mechanism that uses the SQL Server Agent.

Timed transactions in BizTalk Server provide a specific form of scheduling function, whereby an orchestration that is currently suspended while awaiting the arrival of a message will time out after a scheduled period of time.

When an orchestration enters such a wait period, the orchestration is usually dehydrated to the database and then is rehydrated later when the message arrives, or according to the scheduling after a message timeout. In the event of a timeout, the orchestration performs the appropriate exception handling for the timed transaction.

## Contract Management

BizTalk Server provides two key pieces of functionality to support contract management:

- BizTalk Server reliable messaging
- Support for Business Process Execution Language for Web Services (BPEL4WS)

With BizTalk Server reliable messaging, messages that you send to a trading partner are marked up to require a response within a particular time frame.

BizTalk Server can automatically manage both ends of the communication. When BizTalk Server is the originator of the message, it waits for a response from the party to which the message was sent. If there is no message response, it resends the message a configurable number of times. If there is still no response, BizTalk Server marks the message transmission as failed and performs appropriate exception handling.

When BizTalk Server is the receiver of the message, it automatically extracts the return address from the message, formulates a response message, and sends it to the return address specified.

BizTalk Server 2004 also provides full support for BPEL4WS. BizTalk Orchestration provides a superset of BPEL4WS capabilities. In fact, BizTalk Server 2004 can import a BPEL4WS specification from a compliant orchestration and automatically build a compliant orchestration from the specification.

## Data Integration Capabilities

This guide defines a number of capabilities that are required for effective data integration. Table 4.2 shows how Microsoft technologies provide these data integration capabilities.

**Table 4.2: Data Integration Capabilities Provided by Microsoft Technologies**

| Capability | Provided by |
|---|---|
| Data Validation | XML schemas and BizTalk Server parsers |
| Data Access | ADO.NET and SQLXML |
| Schema Definition | BizTalk Editor |
| Data Transformation | SQL Server DTS, XSLT, and BizTalk Mapper |
| Schema Recognition | XML schemas and BizTalk Server parsers |

It is useful to examine these capabilities in more detail.

## Data Validation

Virtually all Microsoft applications support XML technologies centered on the Microsoft implementation of the XML DOM. The DOM defines a standard set of commands that parsers expose so you can access XML document content from your programs. An XML parser that supports the DOM takes the data in an XML document, parses and validates it, and then converts it to a data structure in memory. The data is exposed by way of a set of objects that you can program against. Many Microsoft client applications and server products use the Microsoft XML DOM.

In BizTalk Server, a parser in the receive pipeline performs data validation. The parser component decompiles the message using the information in a supplied schema definition, which is an XSL schema. BizTalk Server provides parsers for XML, custom flat files, and for EDI documents. Each of these parsers uses the XSL schema definition to validate the corresponding document type and convert it to an XML representation.

## Data Access

The .NET Framework includes a new data-access layer that two main groups of classes—the ADO.NET and XML core classes—provide. ADO.NET provides classes that implement database-independent data containers, along with database-oriented tools such as SQL Server and OLE DB commands, managed data providers and connections, data readers, and data adapters. ADO.NET represents the .NET Framework way of working with data, irrespective of data source, data format, or physical location. It also features a data-centric design center that is different from the database-centric vision of ADO and better suited to today's Web programming needs.

SQL Server 2000 was the first version of SQL Server to provide native XML support, which was limited to the more basic XML feature set (template queries, mapping schemas, and OPENXML). The SQLXML add-on provides additional features such as updategrams. SQLXML helps you to build data-driven Web services.

## Schema Definition

You can use the BizTalk Editor (hosted in the Visual Studio integrated development environment [IDE]) to create BizTalk Server schemas. The schema definition specifies the document structure, individual records, and fields that make up the document. For example, the flat-file parser uses the XSL document schema to determine the type of flat-file document (positional, delimited, or some combination of these) and other document features, such as which delimiters and escape characters the document uses. For each field in the document, the XSL schema definition specifies the type (date, integer, string, or other type), and other validation information, such as field lengths.

**Figure 4.1**
*BizTalk Editor*

BizTalk Server provides additional facilities within the IDE that allow you to test schemas against sample instances of those schemas, and to generate sample instances from a schema definition. You can also automatically generate schemas from XML instances, or from XDR schema specifications.

## Data Transformation

SQL Sever DTS provides a set of graphical tools and programmable objects to help you solve data transformation and data movement problems, including how to extract, transform, and consolidate data from disparate sources to single or multiple destinations. Sets of tasks, workflow operations, and constraints can be collected as DTS packages that can be scheduled to run periodically or when certain events occur.

BizTalk Server provides a data transformation mechanism based on XSLT transformations. These transformations are specified as XSLT maps, which convert a source format to a destination format. You can apply maps in either the receive pipeline or the send pipeline, or within an orchestration itself. XSLT maps are developed using the BizTalk Mapper, which also integrates with Visual Studio .NET. Figure 4.2 shows an XSLT map in the BizTalk Mapper interface.

The BizTalk Mapper interface enables you to map source fields to destination fields directly by dragging the source field to the destination field. A large number of data manipulation functions (functoids) can also be applied to the mapping.

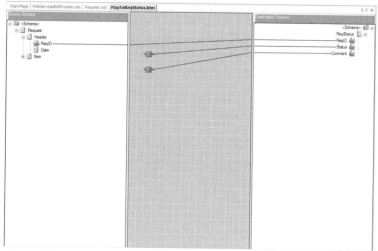

**Figure 4.2**
*XSLT map in BizTalk Server*

Functoids are available from the Visual Studio .NET Toolbox, grouped by type. BizTalk Server provides over 75 functoids, which provide a wide variety of functionality, including the ability to map source fields to different format destination fields, aggregate data (for example, total all the line items in a purchase order), and perform various data lookups (for example, look up a supplier name in a database by supplier ID).

## Communication Capabilities

This guide defines a number of capabilities that are required for effective communication integration. Table 4.3 shows how Microsoft technologies provide these communication integration capabilities.

**Table 4.3: Communication Capabilities Provided by Microsoft Technologies**

| Capability | Provided by |
| --- | --- |
| Message Routing | BizTalk Server MessageBox and subscriptions |
| Message Delivery | BizTalk Server message ports |
| Message Queuing | Microsoft Message Queuing and BizTalk Message Queuing (MSMQT) |
| Message Forwarding | BizTalk Server MessageBox and subscriptions |
| Message Correlation | BizTalk Orchestration correlation services |
| Message Instrumentation | BizTalk Orchestration |
| Addressing | BizTalk Server message ports |

*(continued)*

| Capability | Provided by |
|---|---|
| Transactional Delivery | Microsoft Message Queuing and BizTalk Server reliable messaging |
| File Transfer | BizTalk Server message ports |
| Serialization/Deserialization | BizTalk Server receive and send pipelines |
| Request/Reply | BizTalk Orchestration |
| Batching/Unbatching | BizTalk Server messaging pipelines |
| Encode/Decode | BizTalk Server messaging pipelines |
| Connection Management | BizTalk message ports |

It is useful to examine these capabilities in more detail.

## Message Routing and Message Forwarding

BizTalk Server 2004 provides a publish-subscribe mechanism centered on a feature called the MessageBox. At the time of delivery, a publisher delivering a message to the system for delivery has no knowledge of the message delivery mechanism, or of where (to which receivers) the message will be delivered.

Messages that the system receives are first passed through a receive pipeline. This pipeline preprocesses the message by decoding, decrypting, and so on. In addition, the pipeline extracts additional data about the message and about the message receiving process. For example, it extracts information about what port the message was received on, details of the transport used (for example, what the file name was for a file-based transport), and authentication information (for example, the user ID if available). At the end of this process, the message, together with all the metadata collected about the message, is placed into the MessageBox.

This architecture allows you to implement sophisticated message-addressing and message-routing designs. To route the message to its destination, the MessageBox processing evaluates the subscription rules associated with each outbound port or orchestration port. For each port that has a subscription that matches the metadata, the MessageBox passes a copy of the message to that send or orchestration port. For example, a subscription may be set up that matches all messages received by the ReceivePO receive port.

In addition to routing messages to specific orchestration or messaging ports, you can use the metadata associated with each message to specify addressing information for the eventual destination of the document. Lastly, you can derive the metadata associated with a message from the content of the message, which makes content-based routing very easy to implement.

## Message Delivery

Figure 4.3 (following) shows a high-level overview of message flow within BizTalk Server 2004. Message flow through the system starts at a receive location. BizTalk Server makes a distinction between a receive port (which has a logical representation in the context of the BizTalk Server application being developed), and a receive location (which has a physical representation in the context of the deployed BizTalk Server application).

A receive location specifies a particular transport type (or adapter), various parameters specific to the transport type (for example, the file directory and filename mask), and the pipeline that will be used to process the submitted document. The receive port specifies the authentication and tracking for the receive port, along with any mapping you want to apply to the inbound document. There is a one-to-many relationship between receive ports and receive locations, which means that one receives port can have many different receive locations, spanning multiple different transport types.

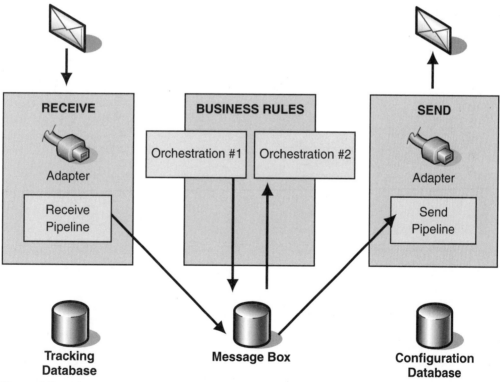

**Figure 4.3**
*Message flow in BizTalk Server 2004*

When a document is submitted to a receive location using an appropriate transport, the message is processed by the pipeline specified for that receive location. A pipeline is a series of logical stages, each of which may be represented by one or more components. The stages in a pipeline represent the processing that the pipeline performs on the document. BizTalk Server comes with several standard receive and send pipelines, with stages to:

- Decode
- Disassemble
- Validate
- Resolve party

You can customize the BizTalk Server generic receive and send pipelines by adding stages. You can also populate each of these stages with one or more custom pipeline components to perform the activities of that stage. For example, to convert a mainframe message encoded with EBCDIC to ASCII, you can write a custom decoding component.

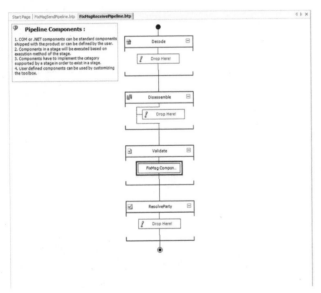

**Figure 4.4**
*Customizing a BizTalk Server pipeline*

After a message is delivered to the MessageBox, it is delivered to each its subscribers. A subscriber to a message is either an orchestration or a send port. An orchestration or a send port sets up a subscription to a message by setting up a message filter, referencing the metadata associated with the message. For example, a send port can set up a filter to receive all messages that were received on a specific receive port.

In addition to send ports, BizTalk Server also uses send port groups, which are collections of send ports. In a BizTalk Server system, each send port can have a subscription, and each port can belong to a send port group. The send port group also has a subscription. When a message is processed, a copy of the message is sent to each subscription in the system that matches the message properties. If the subscription for the send port group matches, the message is sent to each port in the group. If both the send port group and the send port subscriptions match the message properties, the message may be sent to a port twice.

## Message Queuing

BizTalk Server 2004 uses BizTalk Message Queuing (MSMQT) for message queuing, which interoperates transparently with Message Queuing and MQ Series systems. However, the messages are placed directly into the BizTalk Server MessageBox (just as with all other transports) rather than a queue, and BizTalk Server, rather than a queue manager, manages the transport.

## Message Correlation

Previous versions of BizTalk Server provided a mechanism whereby an incoming message was associated with a unique moniker that identified that instance of the business process. This mechanism required you either to place a copy of the unique moniker in the message (which was not always possible) or to write additional code to associate some unique identifier in the message (such as the purchase order number) with the unique moniker of the business process instance.

BizTalk Server 2004 uses a mechanism similar to the latter, whereby you designate some combination of fields in the incoming message as unique (for example, you may designate that the combination of the purchase order number and the purchase order date be guaranteed as unique), and this automatically correlates the message with the correct instance of the business process.

## Addressing

BizTalk Server delivers a copy of a message to any ports where the ports' subscription information matches the message metadata. This mechanism provides a dynamic routing algorithm, which is evaluated at run time, allowing you to develop very sophisticated message routing. In addition, orchestrations that specify ports either can specify all transport information for those ports at development time, or can defer this task until deployment, or at run time.

These send ports or orchestration ports specify the transport involved (which may be a true transport, such as HTTP, or may be an adapter, such as the SQL Server adapter), along with the details of that transport (such as the address). For example, a port may be an HTTP port that sends documents to a specific HTTP address. These addresses can be absolute, or they can be specified using keywords, which are replaced at run time with information from the message metadata.

## Transactional Delivery

As well as providing a sophisticated queuing and message routing infrastructure, Message Queuing also provides transactional message queue support. Hence, Message Queuing provides a resource dispenser, which operates together with the DTC to provide transactional message queues. These queues can be used to implement transactional delivery of messages.

BizTalk Server also provides transactional messages at various levels of integration. Message sent by BizTalk Server are automatically retried if a transport failure (such as an HTTP error response) is returned. When working with Message Queuing, this provides a transactional activity that spans the entire transport process.

For transports that are not transactional (most are not), BizTalk Server also provides a reliable messaging mechanism, where the receiver of a reliable message must reply to that message within a certain time frame, or else the message will be resent. BizTalk Server handles the message retry and receipt automatically.

## File Transfer

BizTalk Server ports manage all transport of messages by using Windows Server messaging services, such as IIS, and the underlying network layer. BizTalk Server supports File, FTP, HTTP, MSMQT, SMTP, SOAP, and SQL Server transports. BizTalk Server does not differentiate between transports such as HTTP and application adapters such as SQL Server 2000. Instead, it handles both types of transport generically as adapters. You can also develop custom adapters to support your file transfer needs.

## Serialization/Deserialization

BizTalk Server uses message processing pipelines to process messages as they are sent and received. A send/receive pipeline commonly has a stage for serializing or deserializing the messages passing through the pipeline. This stage converts the native document from or to XML using a serializer or parser component. BizTalk Server supports XML, custom flat files (both delimited and positional), and EDI document (EDIFACT and X12) parsers. You can build custom serializers or parsers for customized formats, such as HL7 for healthcare applications.

## Request/Reply

Although the underlying communications model is publish-subscribe, you can still accommodate request/reply style models with BizTalk Server. Request/reply is implemented as a request-response port. This implementation is a variation of the standard one-way receive port, which returns a response using the same transport as the received message. Figure 4.5 shows a simple orchestration connected to a request-response port. The orchestration receives a message (through an HTTP Post), performs some processing, and then creates and sends the HTTP response message.

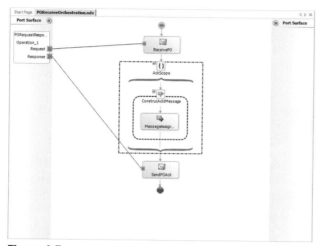

**Figure 4.5**
*Simple BizTalk Server orchestration connected to a request-response port*

You can use similar request-response communication models to implement Web services. In this case, you use orchestration as the implementation mechanism for the Web service.

### Batching/Unbatching

Document batching and unbatching are supported by BizTalk Server, by messaging pipelines, and through use of XML envelopes. A batched message received by BizTalk Server is automatically broken up into its component messages using an envelope that essentially specifies how to unbatch the document. Individual messages are then processed separately by BizTalk Server, and can then be batched up again using a custom pipeline component

### Encode/Decode

BizTalk Server supports document encoding and decoding through the receive and send pipelines. You can decode documents received by BizTalk Server that have been encoded in a specific format (for example EBCDIC from a mainframe, or SMIME for security) within the receive pipeline, prior to processing by BizTalk Server. Similarly, you can encode documents sent from BizTalk Server using an encoding stage in the send pipeline. You can also create custom encoder/decoder pipeline components for use within the pipelines, such as a Pretty Good Privacy (PGP) component.

### Connection Management

BizTalk Server supports a concept of parties taking part in a business process. For example, your organization may do business with numerous suppliers, all of whom receive purchase orders from your organization. You may find that it becomes too complex to manage and administer send ports for each of these suppliers. BizTalk Server solves this problem by implementing the integration application ports in terms of service links.

To add a new trading partner to the application integration solution, you define a new party in terms of the service links required by the application. You specify physical port information for the party, which links to the logical service links.

## Protocol Bridging

Microsoft supports bridging between industry standard protocols (for example, HTTP) and protocols from other vendors by using custom protocol adapters. For example, Microsoft has developed an MQ Series adapter that provides bridging support between Microsoft Message Queuing and IBM MQ Series.

## Security Capabilities

This guide defines a number of capabilities that may be required to secure your application integration environment. Table 4.4 shows how Microsoft technologies provide these security capabilities.

**Table 4.4: Security Capabilities Provided by Microsoft Technologies**

| Capability | Provided by |
|---|---|
| Authorization | Active Directory |
| Authentication | Active Directory and SharePoint Portal Server Enterprise single sign-on |
| Information Protection | Windows Server |
| Identity Management | Enterprise single sign-on |
| Nonrepudiation | Digital signatures |
| Profile Management | Enterprise single sign-on |
| Security Context Management | Active Directory and Enterprise single sign-on |

It is useful to examine these capabilities in more detail.

## Authorization

All resources managed by a Windows Server operating system automatically have authorization checks performed against them whenever a user attempts to access them. The user identity is checked against the access control list of the resource being accessed to determine if the user has the rights to access the resource in that manner. BizTalk Server and all other Microsoft server products use this authorization mechanism.

In addition, you can use Authorization Manager in Windows Server 2003 to facilitate role-based authorization for your applications. Authorization Manager allows you to authorize applications not only against Active Directory, but also against an XML file store.

## Authentication

Users accessing a Windows Server system are required to authenticate. This authentication occurs either as a result of logging on to the network, or for access through a Web-based portal, by authenticating against that portal using standard Web-based authentication methods. Users' security credentials are validated against the credentials maintained for that user in Active Directory.

BizTalk Server manages authentication of users through existing Windows authentication mechanisms. Access to the application integration system itself (for administration, configuration, or for business activity monitoring) requires the user to authenticate himself or herself so that authorization checks can be performed.

For applications or external users submitting documents to BizTalk Server, the kind of authentication available depends on the transport adapter used to receive the message. BizTalk Server supports all common authentication standards for each transport type. For example, when accessing a Web site, authentication occurs through basic authentication, NTLM authentication, certificate-based authentication, or another authentication mechanism.

## Information Protection

Decryption and encryption of messages is managed within the receive and send pipelines by specific encryption pipeline components. These components use the encryption technologies that Windows Server supplies by storing and retrieving digital certificates in the server certificate store, and using these certificates to decrypt or encrypt the documents. You can also write custom pipeline components such as a PGP encryption component.

## Identity Management

When building complex business processes that interact with many systems within the enterprise, you need a mechanism that enables a user to access multiple heterogeneous applications through one enterprise logon. BizTalk Server uses the Enterprise single sign-on (SSO) provided by SharePoint Portal Server. When using SSO, after a user is authenticated by Windows, no additional credentials are required to access resources from non-Windows systems or other back-end systems and applications.

The SSO system is a distributed environment that consists of a centralized credential database and at least one server. The credential database is a SQL Server database that relates the Windows user to the user's corresponding non-Windows credentials. You can also use the SSO system to store additional information, such as receive locations and send ports configuration information that is specific to a user.

### Nonrepudiation

In the same way that business documents can be decrypted and encrypted in the receive and send pipelines, you can use the pipelines to check a received document for a valid digital signature, or to add a digital signature to a document that will be sent to a third-party. Again, this is done by pipeline components, which use Windows Server technologies. Nonrepudiation can be supported by validating the digital signatures fixed to a message and by maintaining the details of the digital signature throughout processing as custom metadata associated with the message.

### Profile Management

BizTalk Server 2004 provides the BizTalk Explorer to streamline partner configuration. You use other BizTalk Server tools, such as Orchestration Designer and Pipeline Designer, to create a single common integration application, and then use BizTalk Explorer to vary the configuration as required for different partners. Decoupling the partner relationship from the business logic in this manner increases the reusability of the solution. You can create an orchestration without knowing the specific send ports or receive locations, which can be configured later. Not only can you reuse orchestrations, but you also have greater flexibility to make changes to the partner relationships without having to change the actual applications.

### Security Context Management

Windows Server requires users to authenticate and performs authorization checks for all resource access. Windows also allows one security context to impersonate another, given appropriate authentication information. Your integration applications can use this feature to access resources in different security contexts.

Similarly, you can use SSO to supply security context information for systems that are not based on Windows. Here, a security principal provides a security context to access the integration application, and then the application obtains another security context from the SSO system.

## Operational Management Capabilities

This guide defines a number of capabilities that may be required for effective operations of your application integration environment. Table 4.5 shows how Microsoft technologies provide these operational management capabilities.

**Table 4.5: Operational Management Capabilities Provided by Microsoft Technologies**

| Capability | Provided by |
| --- | --- |
| Business Activity Management | BizTalk Server Business Activity Monitoring (BAM) |
| Event Handling | Windows Management Instrumentation (WMI) events, Event Viewer, Performance Monitor, and MOM |
| Configuration Management | System Management Server |
| Directory | Active Directory |
| Change Management | BizTalk Server Business Rules Engine and schema versioning |
| System Monitoring | Windows Server and MOM |

It is useful to look at each of these in turn.

### Business Activity Management

SQL Server 2000 Analysis Services is a middle-tier service for OLAP and data mining. Analysis Services includes a server that manages multidimensional cubes of data for analysis and provides client access to cube information. Analysis Services organizes data from a data warehouse into cubes with precalculated aggregation data to provide fast answers to complex analytical queries.

BizTalk Server 2004 uses this technology to track and analyze all documents that are transmitted through a BizTalk Server system. In addition, Analysis Services are used to provide business-level reporting to end users.

Business Activity Monitoring (BAM) in BizTalk Server provides business analysts direct visibility into running business processes. BAM does this by concentrating and analyzing data for heterogeneous information sources, and presenting a real-time view of business state, trends, and critical conditions, enabling them to make better business decisions based on more relevant data.

### Event Handling

All Microsoft server products provide Windows Management Instrumentation (WMI) events, which can be accessed programmatically, or by a variety of client applications. Your business applications can incorporate their own event handling logic (combining this with application specific event handling logic), or you can use one of the many client applications for event handling.

Windows Server includes Event Viewer and Performance Monitor, both of which you can use to view event data for a business application. For more functionality, you can use MOM, which allows you to automatically monitor a wide range of system and application events, and then perform various actions based on the level and severity of the events captured. You can use MOM to monitor events across a large number of servers in an enterprise.

## Configuration Management

Systems Management Server (SMS) 2003 helps you to perform change and configuration management for the Microsoft platform, and gives you the ability to provide relevant software and updates to users. SMS 2003 monitors and manages the installed application base, and allows you to push key updates to servers throughout the enterprise. SMS uses the management capabilities built into the Windows operating system.

In addition, BizTalk Server provides you with a full WMI interface to all BizTalk Server artifacts. The definition for these configuration artifacts can be exported as an XML binding file. You can also recreate the configuration at any time by importing this binding file.

## Directory

Active Directory is the directory service on Windows Server systems. In addition to providing directory services to the operating system itself, Active Directory can be used to provide information to, and store information from custom applications.

## Change Management

BizTalk Server 2004 solutions are deployed as .NET assemblies, which include versioning information. Hence, schemas and maps are all versioned within the assembly that they reside, so when you need to make changes to the system, you manage backward compatibility by referencing specific versions of these components.

Similarly, vocabularies and business rules as deployed by the Business Rules Engine are all fully versioned, so once a business rule has been deployed, it cannot be changed. Instead, a new version of the rule must be created and deployed.

## System Monitoring

BizTalk Server provides monitoring in two separate ways: by writing WMI events and by writing details of all documents processed into the SQL Server database. You can monitor WMI events using various tools supplied with the Windows operating system, such as Performance Monitor and the Event Log, and by using MOM.

MOM provides management of events and performance of Microsoft servers from a Web console. You can create sophisticated rules to respond to events, generate custom reports, or handle operational tasks using one of the add-on management packs. The management packs provide additional information to allow MOM to manage Microsoft servers. For example, BizTalk Server ships with a MOM management pack that defines the key events, and reports required to manage a BizTalk Server system.

You can use the Health and Activity Tracker (HAT) that ships with BizTalk Server to examine all the details of all documents processed, which are captured in the database. This tool essentially provides a (large) number of stored procedures to query specific aspects of the BizTalk Server database. You use the tool to view all messages being processed or that have been processed, and any running orchestrations. Linked to the HAT is an orchestration debugger, which can be configured to stop at any step in an orchestration, and then to step through the orchestration.

# Summary

After you have defined the needs of your application integration environment and determined the capabilities that you require to meet those needs, you should investigate the technologies that you can deploy for application integration. This chapter examined how you can use various Microsoft technologies for application integration, and how these technologies map to the capabilities defined in the appendix.

# Appendix

## Application Integration Capabilities

This appendix provides a detailed description of the capabilities used to support an application integration environment. These application integration capabilities are divided into five categories:

- Business processing
- Data
- Communications
- Security
- Operations

## Business Processing Capabilities

The capabilities defined in this section provide integration at the business processing level.

### Orchestration

The Orchestration capability coordinates the execution of the different activities that make up a business process. Although a business process model is a static representation of the set of activities involved, the Orchestration capability brings the model to life and executes each step within the model. Activities undertaken by the people, systems, or organizations are invoked, coordinated, managed, and measured by the Orchestration capability, according to its process models.

The Orchestration capability triggers the processes corresponding to a business event, passes inputs and outputs across processes, receives communication of status information by different activities, and requests human intervention as necessary.

# Event Processing

Generally, business processes begin either with the arrival of a message from the application integration environment communications capabilities, or they begin with the occurrence of a user action (for example, a user typing a customer's last name and then clicking the Search button in a Web interface). Both are considered events in the context of the application integration environment.

The Event Processing capability recognizes when business events have occurred, logs those events, and determines which business processing capability will receive the event. In most cases, this target is the Rules Processing capability.

The majority of events are expected occurrences, taking place as part of the normal business processing carried out by the environment. However, the Event Processing capability must also handle unexpected events, or exceptions. These exceptions are often the result of system-level events on the computers in the environment. For example, the system-level failure of a database that stores inventory may generate events at the business process level, because the business process of checking and updating inventory is no longer possible. In this case, the application could take tentative orders and warn the user that it is not possible to verify the availability of the product at that time. The same database failure might generate events at other levels as well. At the data level, the orders might be stored in a secondary location until the database could come back online, and at the operations level, actions would be taken to restore the database functionality.

---

System-level events are not handled by the Event Processing capability; instead, they are handled by the Event Handling operational management capability.

---

In your application integration environment, you are likely to have a number of multistep processes, involving multiple applications that are interdependent. This situation can quickly become unmanageable, with a significant number of applications remaining active and simply waiting for responses from other applications that may not come for hours, days, or even months or years. These applications can consume significant processor resources. The State Management capability reduces the impact on your systems by maintaining the following types of state information across different components:

- Process state
- Message state
- Service state

## Process State

Applications that use asynchronous messaging typically run until a message is sent asynchronously to a target application. At that point, the state of the multistep process is normally handed over to the State Management capability, and the application releases its resources and shuts down. When Event Processing recognizes the arrival of the response from the target application, it invokes the State Management capability, which in turn identifies the application that initiated the exchange and restarts that application so that it can receive the response to the original message.

To maintain the state of each of the pending applications, the State Management capability maintains a database with an entry for each pending process. For every pending process, the State Management capability has to store the data that must persist between process steps. Hence, State Management maintains a map of the various process steps with a pointer to the next step in the process (for example, the step that must be executed upon the arrival of the response to the last message sent).

## Message State

Messages exchanged between applications are in various states of processing. Upon arrival, messages are in an active state waiting to be picked up and processed by the receiving application. After they are processed, they are in a journaled state. Messages can also enter the journaled state if they are in the active state for a duration longer than the predefined expiration period. This change of state usually occurs when none of the receiving applications picks up the active message. Journaled messages move on to an archived state when they are archived into a persistent store.

## Service State

To run properly in its target environment, services require multiple pieces of information including user ID, time, date, contents, and any other information the service might need to access. A service that has all the required information is in a state where it is ready to run. Although most of the information is specified as input by the consumer, services may need to collect the remaining information by accessing other systems and data stores. While it is in the process of collecting this information, the service is in a state where it is preparing for execution. After execution, the service is in a dormant state waiting to be invoked by interested consumers.

# Schedule

Not all pending processes simply wait for a response to a message. In some cases, a process is placed in the pending state until a specified time or date, or until a specified amount of time has elapsed. When this time has elapsed (or when the specified date or time is reached), the Schedule capability generates an event for the Event Processing capability just as any other event.

The Schedule capability also acts as a timekeeper, tracking processes where an external event should occur within a specified time frame or by a specified date or time. If this event has not occurred by the specified deadline, an alert or exception is generated and the Event Processing capability passes this alert to the process that was waiting fruitlessly for the expected event.

## Business Transaction Management

Business applications are frequently required to coordinate multiple pieces of work as part of a single business transaction. As an example, think of when you order goods online. Your credit card must be verified, you must be charged, the goods must be selected, boxed, and shipped, and inventory must be managed. All of these steps are interrelated, and if one step fails then generally all of the corresponding steps must be cancelled. The Transaction Management capability coordinates these steps. In some cases, it is not possible to directly cancel out transactions that have already been issued. Instead, you may have to issue additional transactions to compensate for the original transaction. This technique is known as transaction compensation.

## Rules Processing

Several types of rules may be applied in processing data—both to transform the data through the application of an algorithm (for example, a pricing model) and to route the data through application of a set of business rules (for example, orders for widgets are sent to the widget factory that is closest to the Ship To address on the order).

Some of the rules can be asserted at the time of development and require little access to outside systems or data. For example, all of the data needed to process the rule is contained in the message that is passed to the business capability. In other cases, the data needed to process a rule must be pulled from local and remote databases, and from local or remote applications.

The Rules Processing capability enables a developer or a business analyst to specify business rules without writing a lot of procedural code. The rules may be specified in a declarative programming language (for example, one that is not sensitive to arcane punctuation and does not rely on elaborate language constructs). Alternatively, the rules may be specified by answering questions in a graphical environment such as a programming wizard or a sequence of dialog boxes.

Your organization can define a wide range of rules within business processing capabilities, including:

- **Data validation rules**. For example, is this a valid customer number? Is the postal code valid for the city?

- **Processing algorithms.** For example, what is the total price of this order, considering the customer's contract discount and any additional discounts for the size of this order or the number of orders placed this month, and including the costs associated with the custom configuration?

- **Processing rules.** For example, was the customer's insurance policy in effect at the time of the accident? Or is the value of the order large enough to earn free shipping?

- **Sequencing rules.** For example, before the system can approve a second mortgage application, does it need to send a message to a scheduling application to have the house appraised?

- **Exception handling rules.** For example, if you don't have enough widgets in the warehouse, can you order stock from the supplier and have the the supplier ship the order directly to the customer?

- **Non-delivery rules.** For example, if the order isn't acknowledged by the primary supplier within four hours, do you resend the order, call the supplier's expediter, or send the order to a secondary supplier?

- **Prioritization rules.** For example, given the size of the requested insurance policy, do you escalate the request to a senior underwriter, or can a junior underwriter approve the policy?

- **Data reconciliation rules.** For example, since the last batch update of the customer database, the primary contact name for this account has been changed by both the customer service representative and the account executive—to different names. Which update takes precedence (or do you need to call the account executive for clarification)?

This list is not meant to be comprehensive, nor are the rules listed mutually exclusive. However, it is indicative of the range of rules processing requirements that must be supported in an integration solution.

## Workflow

Often, business processing capabilities manage only the interaction between applications, because in many integration scenarios, user interaction is managed only indirectly. That is, the users interact with applications, and the applications in turn interact with the business processing capabilities.

For those processes that do interact directly with users, an additional business processing capability is needed: the Workflow capability. The Workflow capability uses the rules and state management engines to control the interaction between people and the process management environment.

For example, if an "application for fire insurance" event arrives at the process management environment, the Workflow capability may immediately forward the event to an underwriter, who decides whether the applicant should be insured and at what rate.

To ensure that the application is handled by an appropriate underwriter, a set of assignment and escalation rules may be defined and implemented with the help of the rules engine. Perhaps applications that pose no particular problems or risks can be assigned to the Junior Underwriters queue, whereas the riskiest applicants are assigned to the Senior Underwriters queue. In this example, the rest of the applications go in the Underwriters queue.

If the Junior Underwriters queue becomes too long, escalation rules can move up excess applications to the Underwriters queue. Similarly, if the Underwriters queue becomes too long, escalation rules can move up excess applications to the Senior Underwriters queue. However, rules do not permit the reverse to occur; for example, applications cannot be moved down from the Senior Underwriters queue to the Underwriters queue.

In addition to these escalation rules, the Workflow capability may implement prioritization rules. For example, if an application for fire insurance has been sitting in the Underwriters queue for two days, it can be escalated to the beginning of the Senior Underwriters queue so that it can be addressed before some of the new applications in the queue.

## Contract Management

The Contract Management capability monitors and processes contractual obligations at run time. A business contract is an agreement between two or more parties expressing their mutual obligations and permissions for carrying out certain economic exchanges. These exchanges are related to the execution of actions that form multistep business processes.

In the context of business process management, a contract can be treated as a conversation between one party and other parties. The contract can be modeled as one or more workflows where the actions or tasks relevant to the contract (internal to organizations) are described as steps in the parties' business processes. The interactions between parties at various stages of the business process will often take the form of message exchanges.

In a service-oriented architecture, Web services can represent the parties involved in the contract. Specifications such as BPEL4WS can be used to address Web services orchestration and coordination issues. WS-Policy is the emerging standard that is used to implement contract agreements.

# Data Capabilities

The capabilities defined in this section provide integration at the data level.

## Schema Definition

Schemas describe the structure and format of data. Each schema contains property information pertaining to the records and fields within the structure of data. This information is vital to ensuring that the data actually makes sense. Fortunately, in many cases the schema definition already exists and you only need to maintain the definition, rather than redefine the structure of the data.

Schema definitions are presented in a number of different forms in different applications. These forms include well-formed XML, document type definitions (DTDs), Electronic Data Interchange (EDI), and structured document formats. Many predefined schemas in each of these formats may be appropriate for your environment, depending on the applications that you use. For example, hundreds of schemas are associated with the dozens of EDI documents that are defined within each of the multiple versions of the two EDI document standards (X12 and EDIFACT).

You may find it useful to preload schemas from standards organizations, if the schemas are likely to be used in your environment. Sources of such schemas include:

- RosettaNet
- Open Applications Group (OAG)

Other frequently used schema definitions are available from the e-marketplace, including:

- Gas Industry Standards Board (GISB)—used by the energy industry
- Transora—used in e-commerce
- WorldWide Retail Exchange—used in business-to-business scenarios
- Covisint—used in the automotive industry
- Exostar—used in the aerospace and defense industries
- ChemConnect—used in the chemicals, feed stocks, and plastics industries
- FreeMarkets—used in supply management
- E2open—used in process management

In current applications, one of the most commonly used schema definition languages is XML. However, because it is fairly likely that your environment will include applications that do not use XML, you generally should support multiple schema definition languages. Doing so is important in any case to ensure that you support future technologies.

It is also possible to automatically generate XML schemas from data structures such as relational databases, fixed and variable format files, application programming interface specifications, COBOL copybooks, and so on. As well as being much easier, automatically generated schemas are less prone to errors.

Often templates are used for defining common data or documents formats, such as purchase orders, invoices, and shipping notices. The following is an example of a purchase order schema definition:

```xml
<xs:schema xmlns:xs="http://www.w3.org/2001/XMLSchema" targetNamespace="http://
tempuri.org/po.xsd"
xmlns="http://tempuri.org/po.xsd" elementFormDefault="qualified">
 <xs:annotation>
 <xs:documentation xml:lang="en">
  Purchase order schema for Example.com.
  Copyright 2000 Example.com. All rights reserved.
 </xs:documentation>
 </xs:annotation>

 <xs:element name="purchaseOrder" type="PurchaseOrderType"/>

 <xs:element name="comment" type="xs:string"/>

 <xs:complexType name="PurchaseOrderType">
 <xs:sequence>
  <xs:element name="shipTo" type="USAddress"/>
  <xs:element name="billTo" type="USAddress"/>
  <xs:element ref="comment" minOccurs="0"/>
  <xs:element name="items" type="Items"/>
 </xs:sequence>
 <xs:attribute name="orderDate" type="xs:date"/>
 </xs:complexType>

 <xs:complexType name="USAddress">
 <xs:sequence>
  <xs:element name="name"   type="xs:string"/>
  <xs:element name="street" type="xs:string"/>
  <xs:element name="city"   type="xs:string"/>
  <xs:element name="state"  type="xs:string"/>
  <xs:element name="zip"    type="xs:decimal"/>
 </xs:sequence>
 <xs:attribute name="country" type="xs:NMTOKEN"
   fixed="US"/>
 </xs:complexType>

 <xs:complexType name="Items">
 <xs:sequence>
  <xs:element name="item" minOccurs="0" maxOccurs="unbounded">
  <xs:complexType>
   <xs:sequence>
   <xs:element name="productName" type="xs:string"/>
   <xs:element name="quantity">
    <xs:simpleType>
    <xs:restriction base="xs:positiveInteger">
     <xs:maxExclusive value="100"/>
```

```
      </xs:restriction>
      </xs:simpleType>
    </xs:element>
    <xs:element name="USPrice"  type="xs:decimal"/>
    <xs:element ref="comment"  minOccurs="0"/>
    <xs:element name="shipDate" type="xs:date" minOccurs="0"/>
    </xs:sequence>
    <xs:attribute name="partNum" type="SKU" use="required"/>
   </xs:complexType>
   </xs:element>
  </xs:sequence>
  </xs:complexType>

  <!- Stock Keeping Unit, a code for identifying products ->
  <xs:simpleType name="SKU">
  <xs:restriction base="xs:string">
   <xs:pattern value="\d{3}-[A-Z]{2}"/>
  </xs:restriction>
  </xs:simpleType>

</xs:schema>
```

## Schema Recognition

The Schema Recognition capability checks that the schema can be read and understood, and that it is well-formed. The well-formed XML standard dictates that an XML document have a single root and that elements must nest completely or not at all.

Because it is likely that multiple formats will be used for different schemas, it is important that your schema recognition capability be able to accept multiple schema formats. After a schema is recognized and registered, subsequent data can be received and checked for compliance to the corresponding schema.

The Schema Recognition capability also performs schema validation. Schema validation is the verification that the schema definition conforms to a predefined document structure (for example, a DTD).

## Mapping

Data is often rendered in different formats in source and target applications. The relationship between two applications and how the data must be transformed from the source to the target is handled by the Mapping capability.

As you define your mapping capability, you should consider both the development (or design-time) component, and the run-time component. For development, the mapping capability should enable developers to specify the mapping logic in a declarative, nonprocedural way—for example, using the mouse to delineate the mapping between a field in the source data structure and the position of that data in the target data structure. At run time, the mapping capability should be able to access reference data (for table lookups) and perform other data enrichment functions, such as sorting and filtering multiple input records before creating an output data set.

Two forms of mapping can be performed:

- Field mapping
- Semantic mapping

The following paragraphs discuss each mapping type in turn.

### Field Mapping

Field mapping is a data translation process in which the records and fields in the source specification are related to their corresponding occurrences in the destination specification. When data is moved between different applications, several levels of transformation may be required.

In some cases, each field that is moved from the source to the target representation has to be converted. Maybe the source application allows mixed case, but the target application accepts only uppercase. Or maybe the source application allows additional characters (such as dashes or spaces) for formatting purposes.

Often, the data can be converted by applying a straightforward conversion algorithm (for example, temperatures can be converted from Celsius to Fahrenheit through a simple calculation). In other cases, though, the transformation may require a table lookup and replacement (for example, converting the gross weight of a product to net weight may require a lookup based on the product code).

### Semantic Mapping

As data is moved from one application to another, the data structure itself may need to be modified. This modification is known as semantic mapping.

As an example of semantic mapping, consider the different ways of representing addresses. Table A.1 shows two separate applications storing the same address information, but in a different structure.

**Table A.1: Different Ways of Storing Address Information**

| Application 1 | Example | Application 2 | Example |
|---|---|---|---|
| Address 1 | One Microsoft Way | Number | One |
| Address 2 | | Street | Microsoft Way |
| Town | Redmond | City | Redmond |
| State/Province | WA | State and ZIP Code | WA 98052 |
| ZIP/Postal Code | 98052 | | |

Moving data between these two representations requires shuffling the data elements around a bit, but care must be taken so that none of the semantic values of the data (in other words the meaning of the data) is lost as a result of this reorganization of the data elements.

## Data Validation

Data requirements for an enterprise change over time. You may have preexisting systems in your environment that produce data that is not of the quality that the business now requires. Or a change in business context may mean that data that was once correct is now incorrect. The Data Validation capability can verify that data meets the criteria you set and is therefore useful to transfer between applications. The complexity of the validation depends on the enterprise business rules and the capabilities of the application integration tool itself. However, Table A.2 gives some examples of what to expect.

**Table A.2: Example Data Validation Rules**

| Data validation rule | Example |
| --- | --- |
| Syntax validation | Alphabetic characters appear only in alphabetic fields. |
| Semantic validation | A date field actually holds a date. |
| Format validation | A date field requires dates in the U.K. date format (24/03/2001). |
| Range validation | A field requires a number in the range from 10 to 10000. |
| Dependency validation | A field must contain a certain value when another field contains a certain value. |
| Mandatory validation | A field must contain a value. |
| Size validation | A field must be 20 characters long. |
| Value set validation | A value in the field must be M or F (as in Male or Female). |
| Count validation | There cannot be more than one Employee ID for each employee. |

## Data Transformation

The Data Transformation capability is the capability that actually renders the content of input data elements to the corresponding elements of the output data as specified in the map. Data Transformation works in conjunction with the Mapping capability to ensure that not only is data sent to the correct location, but that it is in the right form when it arrives. The Data Transformation capability performs a number of important tasks, including:

- Data aggregation/disaggregation
- Data enrichment

- Data summarization
- Data filtering

The following paragraphs discuss each of these tasks in turn.

### Data Aggregation/Disaggregation

Some data must be merged together before it can be sent. Data may need to be combined from multiple applications, or from a single application over time. The Data Transformation capability uses the Mapping capability to identify the data to be merged and composes new data out of elements of the input data. The map tells the Data Transformation capability where the data elements come from.

Data aggregation may be required to perform both transactional (one record-at-a-time) transformation and batch, set-oriented transformation. For nearly real-time or real-time transactional transformation, the Data Transformation capability may wait for the arrival of messages from several applications and then combine that data to create a single output message. Or, the Data Transformation capability may receive a message and then more proactively request the additional data elements from other applications.

Data aggregation is often constrained by the Rules Processing capability, which monitors the composition process and examines the integrity of the composed message.

Data disaggregation is the opposite of data aggregation. Specific data may need to be broken up into several pieces of output data. Semantic mapping specifies the output data, and data disaggregation decomposes the input data into the output data.

### Data Enrichment

When input data is being formatted into output data, the input data may not hold all of the information that is required for output data. The Data Transformation capability enables you to specify where to acquire the information to enrich the output data. In many cases, this information is acquired from a data store. The Data Transformation capability may use the Data Access capability to look up this information source.

### Data Filtering

The Data Transformation capability provides a mechanism with which users can filter out information from specific data. There may well be an occasion when it is either difficult to filter the information at the source, or when the filter should only be applied to certain targets. Applying the filter to certain targets is very important when you want to filter out sensitive information that a business user does not want to send to certain partners. Data filtering is also used to disseminate predefined cross-sections of data from source applications to target applications across multiple channels. Using data filtering can prevent you from having to change the source application, which may save significant effort and maintenance costs.

# Data Access

As data is being passed from application to application, often different collections of the data are required by each application. One important consideration is how you take the data that already exists and optimize the process of accessing that data. There are three choices to consider for data access:

- Dynamic data access
- Staged data access
- File/database access

The following paragraphs discuss each of these data access choices in turn.

### Dynamic Data Access

Integration solutions are often best served by dynamically creating business objects, where a business object contains all of the required data to be accessed by a business process. The Data Access capability creates these business objects when source data is published or when a request arrives from a composed or straight-through processing (STP) application.

### Staged Data Access

In some occasions, creating data for access dynamically isn't the best approach. For example, when the data collection process has an unacceptable impact on the response times of the applications that are being accessed (specifically, the response times for the regular users of the source applications), the integration solution has to be adjusted so that the impact on these users is less troublesome.

Similarly, response times for the STP or composed application may be unacceptable. For example, suppose that you are building a composed application and that collecting the data required to meet users' needs will involve sequential access to ten applications, each with a response time of two seconds. The two-second response time for each individual application is quite acceptable to most users. However, the cumulative response time of 20 seconds is not acceptable.

These performance issues can be addressed by placing the data into a separate database, called a staged data set. A platform for staging data (using some intermediate data format) is useful for those integration scenarios where the data from the source applications can't be accessed directly and immediately from the source applications.

Putting data into a staged data set is a straightforward process when the data is stable and when the access from the integration programs is read-only. However, if the source applications update the data on a regular basis, those updates have to be propagated from the source applications to the staged data set within a short time frame. Otherwise, the data will become stale and less useful to the integration programs. The reverse problem is also a possibility. If the integration programs are going to change the data in the staged data set, then those changes have to be propagated to the source applications in a short time frame.

### File/Database Access

In addition to accessing data from applications, data stored in flat or structured files as well as databases need to be retrieved for processing. Most file and database access mechanisms are programmatic.

# Communications Capabilities

The capabilities defined in this section provide integration at the communications level.

### Request/Reply

The Request/Reply capability facilitates synchronous communication between applications. In request/reply interactions, the source application sends a request to the target and then performs no other processing until the reply is received.

Request/Reply does not normally use queuing because the requestor is waiting for a reply. Instead, a timeout parameter is set. If the reply is not received in a certain amount of time, the requester resends the request.

Request/Reply also uses other capabilities in the environment to provide its functionality. For example, the Directory capability can resolve addresses for the Request/Reply capability.

To enable request/reply interaction between two applications, a common data format is required as well as common data and process semantics.

### Connection Management

When a request/reply interaction takes place, the Connection Management capability establishes a logical connection between the requesting and the replying applications. Connection Management assigns a connection ID to both applications and then returns the reply to the application that sent the request.

### Message Routing

The Message Routing capability controls the routing of messages from source to target applications. Message routing is a quite simple problem when it entails moving the data from Point A to Point B. In other conditions, however, the routing process can be quite elaborate—for example, when moving the data from Point A to a hub, where the message may be forwarded to Points B, C, or D, based on a variable such as time of day, server load, or message content.

The message itself is a formal construct containing the data. You can think of the message format as an envelope, with the contents of the envelope being routed based on the addressing information that is listed on the outside of that envelope. In practice, the addressing information is often placed in a message header and the content of the message then follows the header in the message's data structure.

The routing functionality is built into the message hub, which inspects each message in sequence, determines where to send the message, and then sends it to the target system.

## Addressing

Your application integration environment cannot route messages correctly unless it can determine where to send the messages. The Addressing capability maintains the information about where to route the message. The environment can determine the location of the target system(s) through either direct or indirect addressing.

### Direct Addressing

Direct addressing is used when the source application specifies the target application for communication. The source application may either specify a network address or a name, that the Addressing capability in turn resolves to a network address, through a call to the Directory capability.

### Indirect Addressing

Indirect addressing occurs when the source application does not specify a target application. Instead, the Addressing capability determines the correct target application after the message has left the source application.

There are two forms of indirect addressing: publish/subscribe addressing and content-based routing.

#### Publish/Subscribe Addressing

In publish/subscribe addressing, the source application sends out the message without indicating the target application; the identity of the target application may not even be known to the source application or its developer. Instead of a destination address, the source application identifies each message by providing a topic name.

Independent of the activities of the source application, potential target applications register with the Addressing capability when they are initialized. During this registration, each target application indicates that it is interested in receiving all messages on a specified topic.

Publish/subscribe addressing provides a useful anonymity to sources and targets, meaning that applications can be added or removed at any time. At run time, the messages are published by the source application(s) with topic names, and the Addressing capability builds a routing table automatically to route each message to the target application(s) that had previously subscribed to messages about the topic. Published messages are often kept in a data store for access by subscribers.

### Content-Based Routing

Content-based routing is closely related to publish/subscribe addressing. In content-based routing, the source application again does not specify the target application's identity. However, content-based routing differs from publish/subscribe addressing in that a developer builds a routing table that specifies rules to determine the correct match between a particular message and a target application. For example, the table may ensure that all orders for a certain product go to the factory that makes that product.

## Message Forwarding

Sometimes a message must be passed through several applications before a response to the original request can be completed. The Message Forwarding capability handles such serial messages.

The forwarding capability can also serve another purpose. In some integration implementations, several intermediaries are needed to provide message management and monitoring capabilities. In such cases, Message Forwarding moves the data between each of the intermediaries, while keeping track of the required sequence.

## Message Delivery

The Message Delivery capability determines how messages pass from source application to target application. Message Delivery occurs through one of two mechanisms: multicasting or single casting.

### Multicasting

Message delivery through multicasting involves delivering the same message to all (or nearly all) of the potential target applications and letting them decide whether to keep the message or not.

The multicasting approach may seem rather wasteful of bandwidth. In reality, however, most local networks are Ethernet-based, which works according to a similar principle, so the multicasting approach does not lead to excess traffic on these networks. In fact for transmission over local area networks (LANs), multicasting is often the most efficient form of message delivery.

Of course, the vast majority of networks consist of multiple LANs. In situations where the message is intended for addresses on other LANs, gateways are used to forward the multicast message to the LANs where the remote addresses reside. Most integration scenarios involve the bridging of several LANs with message delivery gateways.

### Single Casting

Message delivery through single casting involves delivering each message to specific targets as identified by the Addressing capability. Single casting is not always the most efficient way of sending messages, because addresses have to be resolved before they can be sent to each recipient, which can slow performance. However, single casting is very useful in some circumstances; for example, when a number of intermediaries perform routing, filtering, and forwarding functions on the message.

## Message Queuing

In application integration, it is often important to provide guaranteed delivery of each message to ensure that the message reaches its recipient. It is also important that each message is delivered once and only once to its destination. Otherwise, it would be easily possible, for example, for a customer to receive multiple shipments of goods when he or she placed only one order. Finally, it is important that the messages arrive at their destination in the order in which they were sent. This ensures that, for example, an order correction does not arrive before the order that it is correcting.

The implementation of reliable messaging depends on the Message Queuing capability. This capability stores each message in a queue until it can be successfully delivered.

This queue can be implemented in memory or on disk. Implementing this queue in memory can maintain high performance, but at the risk of losing messages if the server fails. Disk implementations trade off higher reliability for slower performance because disk I/O is required every time the message metadata has to be updated to reflect completion of another step in the guaranteed delivery process.

When a message is not delivered successfully, it remains in a queue, and the Message Delivery capability attempts to redeliver the message. After attempting delivery a set number of times at a set interval (as defined by an administrator), the Message Delivery capability places any messages that cannot be delivered in a dead letter queue. Administrators can inspect the dead letter queue, and correct a message addressing header or message content to ensure successful retransmission to the intended destination.

At this point, a message may also have to be sent to the source application to indicate this failure. Or, a message may be sent to an administrator who can help determine the source of the addressing error.

## Message Instrumentation

Although messages are sent in a specific order, they can be received in any order. The Message Instrumentation capability helps ensure that the messages are processed in the order that was originally intended.

The correct order can be ensured by using sequence numbers on the messages themselves. In this case, Message Instrumentation adds the sequence numbers and accepts messages only if the previous message has been correctly received. It may also add the name of each intermediate hub to every message along with a time stamp as it reaches each hub. This additional information enables you to create historical reports on messages and may assist in resolving any performance issues.

## Message Correlation

In an asynchronous interaction, there is no logical connection between the sending and receiving applications. When the receiving application replies to the initial transmission, the receiving application has to specify the proper application name or network address along with the reply message.

Because an application may send several messages asynchronously before receiving a reply for any of them, the application that sends asynchronous messages uses the Message Correlation capability to match up or correlate each reply with the corresponding transmission. Each time a message is sent or received, the Message Correlation capability is called so that it can append a tracking number to the message header. In terms of functionality, this mechanism is very similar to the Connection Management capability used in synchronous messaging.

## Serialization/Deserialization

Data often exists in a hierarchical format in applications. However, as it travels between applications, data must be converted into a flat structure so that it can be sent over the network. The Serialization capability does this conversion. Of course, after the data arrives at its destination, it must also be converted from a flat structure back into its original hierarchical structure. The Deserialization capability does this conversion.

## Transactional Delivery

Often, you must guarantee the delivery of messages. The Transactional Delivery capability groups together messages, sending and receiving them within a transaction. This means that such messages either are sent together in order (a committed transaction), or are not sent at all (an aborted transaction). Likewise, transactional messages are only read (removed) from a queue if and when the transaction is committed. Otherwise, they are returned from a queue and can be subsequently read during another transaction.

The Transactional Delivery capability ensures that transactions meet the following requirements, known collectively as ACID (Atomicity, Consistency, Isolation, and Durability), which are defined as follows:

- *Atomicity* refers to the need to complete all the parts of the transaction or none of them. For example, when a pick list is generated to take a book from the shelf, the inventory quantity for that book should be decreased.

- *Consistency* refers to the need to maintain internal consistency among related pieces of data. For example, in a funds transfer application in a bank, a $100 withdrawal from a customer's savings account should be completed successfully only if a corresponding $100 deposit is made in that customer's checking account.

- *Isolation* refers to the need to ensure that the activities within one transaction are not mixed with the actions of parallel transactions. For example, if five simultaneous requests for a particular book arrive and the warehouse has only four copies of the book in stock, the five transactions must each run in isolation so that the orders are processed properly. Otherwise, it might be possible for each of the five business transactions to see an inventory level of five books and then try to reduce the number to four.

- *Durability* refers to the need to ensure that the results of the transaction are changed only by another valid transaction. The results of the transaction should not be compromised by a power outage or system failure.

To assist in providing durability, your transactional delivery mechanism could employ a disk-based delivery method, where every message is written to permanent storage as it moves through the system. However, to provide durable transactions, the message must be committed to a persistent storage the moment the transaction is completed.

---

**Note:** To overcome system unavailability, you can use persistent messaging as an alternative to Transactional Delivery. Persistent messaging makes the message itself more resilient.

---

Transactional Delivery has a performance cost, because of the overhead involved in ensuring that delivered messages can be rolled back, or in resending messages after a delivery failure. However, the performance tradeoff is often necessary to provide additional guarantees during message delivery.

## Batching/Unbatching

You may not always have continuous, fast, and reliable network connections throughout your enterprise. It can therefore be very useful to collect messages and then send them when the link is available. The Batching/Unbatching capability provides this functionality.

One of the disadvantages of a batching and unbatching approach to communications is that it can lead to unacceptable inconsistencies in data. For example, the same object can be deleted from a database in two separate locations, but there may be no realization that this has occurred until the batch processes take place later.

## Encode/Decode

Different operating systems use different character encoding methods for representing text characters. For example, IBM mainframe applications use Extended Binary-Coded Decimal Interchange Code (EBCDIC) as a character encoding method, while other systems either use ASCII or Unicode. The Encode/Decode capability is responsible for ensuring that applications can still communicate, despite using different encoding methods.

Even when two systems use the same encoding method, there may be differences in the actual encoding due to the use of different code pages. These different code pages are necessary because many languages use different alphabets. Some vary in minor ways (for example, Spanish uses a character constructed by placing a tilde above the character "n"). Others are radically different (for example, the Romance and Germanic languages use the Latin or Roman alphabet, whereas languages such as Arabic, Hebrew, Japanese, and Korean use entirely different alphabets).

When communication capabilities receive the data, the Decode capability is invoked as necessary to convert the data to the encoding method and code page used by the components of the integration solution. This decoding ensures that integration functions such as transformation and routing can be properly performed. After the integration middleware is ready to transmit a message to the target system(s), the message may have to be recoded by using the encoding system and code page of the target system(s).

## File Transfer

In some cases, rather than using request/reply or message-based communication, applications must communicate by exchanging files over the network. The File Transfer capability handles this process of moving or transmitting files between applications.

File Transfer can be useful in an environment when applications are not designed to communicate with other applications directly, but are designed to read, manipulate, and create files. You may also use the File Transfer capability in conjunction with the Batching/Unbatching capability to collect messages into a file, and then transfer that file at a particular time or date, or when a reliable communications link to the target system is available.

Although file transfer lacks some of the sophistication of other communication capabilities, it is still a widely used communication mechanism, due to the number of applications that read and write to files as their only way of communicating. One advantage of file transfer over messaging-based communications is that this type of communications usually is possible within a simpler infrastructure than messaging.

# Security Capabilities

The capabilities defined in this section help provide security to your application integration environment.

## Authentication

As a user or system attempts to connect to another system, the user or system generally presents a set of credentials. The process of verifying those credentials is known as authentication.

Authentication is one of the most fundamental aspects of IT security, because it verifies the identity used to connect, and the security context of the connection. There are many possible methods of authentication, but the most commonly used today is a name and password combination. This method is popular because it is quite quick to implement; however, because this type of authentication is generally custom implemented, the level of security and interoperability really depends on the design and implementation.

To increase the security of authentication itself, it is necessary to encrypt the credentials through a network authentication protocol. The Kerberos authentication protocol is commonly used because it is supported by both UNIX and the Microsoft® Windows® operating system (Windows 2000 and later). Kerberos is a network authentication protocol, defined by the Internet Engineering Task Force (IETF), that relies on public key cryptography. However, the use of Kerberos for authentication with third parties requires trust relationships to be established and access to the Kerberos key distribution center. The Kerberos key distribution center is where the private keys of *principals* (users or systems) are kept for encrypting information.

For more information about the Kerberos protocol, see RFC1510 (*http://www.ietf.org /rfc/rfc1510.txt*).

## Authorization

Authorization is the process of determining whether a particular connection attempt should be allowed. It occurs after authentication, and uses the identity confirmed in authentication to determine if a connection attempt should be permitted.

Authorization can be used to restrict the systems that can request integration capabilities. Such restriction is useful if your organization requires strict control on which systems can use its capabilities. A number of existing authentication protocols, including Kerberos, also provide authorization capabilities. Kerberos relies on a ticketing mechanism; after authentication, the principal is provided with a unique ticket. This ticket can have an access control list (ACL) attached to it. The ACL is used to determine the resources that the principal can access.

## Identity Management

It is quite common for a single user or system to have multiple sets of credentials that are used to access different systems. The Identity Management capability allows you to manage these credentials and map them to the correct user or system.

Identity Management is particularly important for effective application integration, because it allows single sign-on (SSO). This means that if a user needs to be authenticated, the sign-on should be required only once per session, with the appropriate credentials being used to authenticate the user in other environments.

Single sign-on for user authentication is an important convenience for users and can also save time in application integration scenarios by reducing the amount of human interaction. Identity Management is equally important when applications are making the requests, because it ensures that the correct credentials are passed to the capability. Without an identity management system, this programming logic would need to be built into each application.

The two common identity storage implementations for a single system rely either on a Directory capability application or on custom application logic, which in turn relies on a relational database system.

**Note:** Identity management functionality can be provided out of the box with an identity management product. Custom implementation of this technique requires proper security threat analysis to prevent security holes through which unauthorized users or applications can access a capability by assuming the identity of an authorized user or application.

## Security Context Management

Authentication and authorization allow a user or application to communicate with an integration capability. However, when that capability accesses the underlying applications, it must in turn provide credentials to those applications. This management of credentials is achieved by the Security Context Management capability.

Security Context Management provides credentials to applications through two methods:

- **Impersonation**. The integration capability impersonates, or assumes the identity of, the original requester when accessing the underlying applications. The actual credential used for authentication with the back-end applications can be the original credentials provided, or the Security Context Management capability can obtain the appropriate credentials from the Identity Management capability.

- **Consolidation**. The integration capability uses a single identity to access the underlying application. Consolidation grants the same permissions to all requesters that can enter the capability. Consolidation is commonly used for composed applications because it provides simple user management to the existing systems and a better opportunity to pool connections. Connection pooling can improve system performance and is commonly implemented for database access. The benefit of connection pooling is minimal when the request is quite small, compared to the overhead of setting up a connection to the existing application to initiate the communication. However, when you need to transmit a significant amount of data across a network, pooling connections can improve performance dramatically.

## Profile Management

Profile Management manages principal profiles. Generally, applications use principal profiles to provide customization that is specific to the principal accessing the system. The profile management system can store and manage information such as user roles. Given that the Identity Management capability keeps track of the principal identity, the system commonly stores additional information, such as profiles for the principal. This allows the profile information to be extracted at the time of authentication and authorization, which in turn allows efficient use of resources.

## Information Protection

There are essentially three ways that systems can protect information:

- Encryption
- Hashing
- Obfuscation

The following paragraphs discuss each of these information protection methods in turn.

### Encryption

Data is encrypted to prevent unauthorized users from easily viewing or tampering with it. A common encryption technique relies on a secret key system, in which the sender uses a secret key to encrypt the data, and the recipient must provide a corresponding key to decrypt the data. In the context of application integration, secret key encryption is probably the most commonly used form of encryption.

One of the biggest issues with secret key encryption is the requirement for the sender and recipient of the data to know the same secret key. The more parties involved in the communication chain, the more places to which the secret key must be distributed and the greater the risk that the key may become tainted. The encrypted data is usually tied to the exact key used to encrypt the information. If the key is changed, existing encrypted data must be decrypted and reencypted with the new key.

Another method of encrypting data is known as the public key system. A public key system uses two types of keys: private and public. The private key is kept by the owner of the key, whereas the public key can be widely distributed. Data is encrypted using the public key, and the same information can only be decrypted using the private key. Parties wanting to use public key encryption must have the recipient's public key to be able to encrypt the data. Another important feature of this system is the ability to sign data. Signed data can be viewable during transmission, so it is not encrypted. The idea behind signing is to ensure that the actual data has not been altered. Signing essentially uses the hashing technique on the data.

Public key encryption relies on digital certificates, which are files containing a unique (cryptographically generated) sequence of letters and numbers. Public key encryption uses a public certificate and a private certificate representing the public and private keys, respectively. The use of and access to the private keys usually requires a password, so in effect there are two layers of protection. The downside of public key encryption is that it requires additional infrastructure support. This infrastructure, commonly referred as public key infrastructure (PKI), consists of the following protection mechanisms:

- **Hashing**. Hashing, also known as one-way hash, generates a hash value for data. This hash value provides a unique identification for the information, similar to fingerprints. Hashed information cannot be retrieved from the hash value, because the hash value does not carry the original information. Identity management systems commonly store the hash values of passwords so that the actual user password is never stored and so that no one other than the user knows the real password value. The system simply hashes the password given during authentication; if the hashed value matches the hash value stored, then the user must have provided the same password value because hash algorithms provide statistically unique hash values.

- **Obfuscation**. Obfuscation describes a protection mechanism using a simple algorithm that does not rely on user-defined keys. In effect, the information is encrypted, however, if the algorithm is known, any user can decrypt the information. Obfuscation is normally used to protect program codes. Higher-level languages such as C++, the Microsoft Visual Basic® development system, Java, and C# ultimately compile to machine code. Java and Microsoft .NET compile to a more user-friendly code that makes reverse engineering slightly simpler. Obfuscation attempts to make it difficult for reverse-engineered programs to be easily understood.

**Note:** For key based encryptions and hashing, the algorithm used can be well known. However, the data is still protected because it relies on unique keys to protect the data. Obfuscation, on the other hand, does not rely on keys; it relies on the obfuscator algorithm to secure the data, which means that when the algorithm is known, the information can usually be easily decoded.

## Nonrepudiation

Nonrepudiation describes the ability for a party to be identified without ambiguity through digital signatures. The idea behind nonrepudiation is similar to the use of signatures on credit cards. Credit card signatures are meant to allow the authorized user to verify his or her identity and, more importantly, to prove that the user authorized the charge.

Credit card fraud is common because thieves can forge the cardholder's signature. In the digital world, nonrepudiation currently relies on public key encryption, although it has been suggested that a combination of public key encryption and biometrics would enhance security. It is important to stress that for public key encryption the level of security increases with the size of the key or the number of certificates. Currently, the most common key size is 128 bits. It is estimated that to decode 128-bit encrypted information using the most powerful computer today would take 1 trillion years. Obviously as computers become more powerful, the key size will need to be increased to provide additional protection.

Technologies such as Digital Rights Management essentially use the public key encryption mechanism of data protection to provide nonrepudiation. Digital Rights Management controls the access and distribution of digital information. However, no consistent and universal system currently exists that allows particular information to be restricted to certain users for certain periods of time. For example, when an e-mail message is sent, the information it contains is outside the sender's control. The recipients can copy or forward the message to anyone. Digital Rights Management can help by allowing the sender to restrict copying or forwarding to other people who have not been given explicit rights to view the message.

# Operations Capabilities

The capabilities defined in this section provide operations functionality to your application integration environment.

## System Monitoring

System Monitoring includes the monitoring of hardware, the operating system, and software applications to ensure that these various system components are functioning correctly and within the desired operating parameters or agreed-upon capability levels.

One of the most fundamental and often ignored aspects of monitoring is the concept of baselining. Every system behaves uniquely in terms of how quickly it responds to certain requests and the amount of resources it consumes to satisfy requests. It is very important to obtain baseline values for each of the metrics being monitored.

Baselining establishes a standard against which future comparisons can be made to detect anomalies.

There are several ways of viewing what a baseline really means, depending on the maturity of the system being monitored. For a newly commissioned system or a system receiving a major upgrade, it is useful to be able to obtain a baseline value based on a single transaction for each of the different transaction types. As the system matures, you may find it helpful to establish a different set of baselines based on other metrics that make sense for your application. For example, you may create a new baseline, measured only on working days to reflect the fact that systems exhibit certain load characteristics based on the working days of the week. Baselining can also be extended to the provisioning of capabilities and the associated time and cost involved. Baselines can help you to estimate the cost and time involved in extending the existing capability (through scaling up or scaling out) to handle larger loads.

## Event Handling

Event handling can be classified into two categories: passive and active.

Passive event handling is commonly found in applications. It basically receives the event and logs or display the information. The system does not attempt to understand the exception type and resolve it.

Active event handling requires the capabilities of passive exception handling, but provides the additional capability to process and attempt to resolve the issue that caused the exception.

A resilient integration application provides some capabilities of active event handling. This allows minor exceptions to be automatically handled and allows the requests to go through as normal. A very simple example is a system that tries to access another back-end system through an unreliable network connection and as a result may lose requests. The integration application can build a timeout mechanism such that it can automatically retry if the first request fails.

## Business Activity Management

Business Activity Management is an important aspect of any integration system. However, the term Business Activity Management is broad. In the context of this discussion, you should consider Business Activity Management as the monitoring, managing, and analysis of business transactions processed by the integration system.

Activity monitoring enables real-time tracking of business transactions. Alerting of business exceptions is an important feature of monitoring because it enables business analysts to react to any problems with business transactions as they occur. Fixing problems before users notice them, or being able to at least notify users in advance of potential delays, is a key part of proactive monitoring. Examples of problems can range from systems being unavailable to particular steps of the process exceeding the maximum allowed processing time. The latter is important for businesses that must adhere to business capability-level agreements with their customers or partners.

Activity management enables a business analyst to react to a business exception by modifying the transaction process path in real time, before the system rejects the transaction. Actual modification of predefined business processes is considered part of the development and application release process, due to the more permanent nature of the changes.

Activity analysis is about capturing all of the business transaction information that has passed through the system. All data that is relevant to the business transaction —such as process step response times, business data values, and data sources—is captured and is placed in a data warehouse. This allows the business analyst to perform historical analysis of the business process steps from numerous aspects. This ability is extremely important for process-oriented businesses that have capability-level agreements with customers or partners. Having this information allows the business to quickly verify whether it has breached any capability-level agreements. For example, imagine that a parts supplier has agreed with various business partners to process any orders and provide an invoice along with delivery tracking within three days from the time the order is received. If the integration system handles the whole process, it will be able to capture the duration of any process steps as well as the end-to-end processing time. Each step may involve other systems, or it may involve humans who approve or perform further processing. If the partners complain that the business constantly misses its processing-time commitments, the business can then perform an analysis and determine the reason for the delays. Similarly, having the right monitoring in place allows warnings to be generated if a particular step has exceeded its maximum processing time.

## Configuration Management

For the purposes of this guide, configuration management refers to the tracking of hardware and software configurations. Although most configuration management tasks focus on process and documentation, a number of technology capabilities can assist in this area.

**Note:** This guide does not cover asset management.

Configuration management is important for a number of reasons. One of the most important is that it helps you keep track of how each system is configured. This information is very advantageous to have for disaster recovery scenarios. Another benefit of configuration management is that it helps you to compare two systems and to verify them before and after you make modifications, such as application upgrades. It is quite common for systems to exhibit stability issues for no apparent reason, but then on investigation to reveal that some of the files have been replaced or modified to different versions.

Being able to track dependencies is another important part of configuration management. Properly maintained dependency information can provide a real benefit in the area of change management, especially when determining possible impacts of a particular change and what regression testing might need to be performed.

## Versioning

Versioning forms an important part of configuration management. Versions allow you to quickly verify whether the application or operating system files are correct. They can also help you to determine whether your applications have backward or forward compatibility.

---

**Note:** Effective versioning requires technology and policy support. It is important to ensure that version guidelines are defined and followed.

---

It is possible for applications to detect version information and enforce policies that determine which particular version of libraries can be used with the current version of the application. This mechanism ensures that either the application runs as expected or that it fails right away, if the required version of the libraries is not available.

Signing the actual binary images in conjunction with versioning provides an additional layer of protection and verification, which can be important when ensuring if certain files have been modified due to virus infection or malicious acts.

Some of the most commonly changed information is configuration data, which administrators often use a text editor to change. Signing the configuration file allows changes to the configuration information to be detected.

Integration applications may also keep a recent history of the configuration file, or upon loading a new configuration file may generate a log highlighting the changes between the newly loaded version and the version currently used. This mechanism allows specific attributes to be tracked and easily identified, simplifying trouble-shooting problems related to errors in configuration.

## Automated Provisioning

One of the most common issues with manual configuration is human error. It is the main reason that large organizations create images or automated system provisioning systems to reduce the amount of human involvement. Systems are usually composed of a variety of applications, software patches, and hardware. Even when the same applications are installed on two systems, if they were installed in a different sequence, some aspects of the configuration may be different. Such situations can produce problems that are difficult to discover. Automated provisioning of the base system and applications helps to ensure consistency between systems and platforms.

### System Configuration Snapshot

A system configuration snapshot provides the ability to capture a snapshot of the system when changes were made. Such a snapshot essentially provides a mini backup capability, which allows the system to be rolled back when the changes produce undesired results. Without a system configuration snapshot, the usual course of action is to revert to a backup of the system.

Using the snapshot information, you can also compare the system to provide a before-and-after view and to track and control exact changes.

### Configuration Verification

It is very important for you to be able to identify and verify the configuration of your systems .If you cannot, configuration of any system is at the mercy of the quality of provisioning and change management. When something goes wrong, it is difficult to check whether the configuration has been modified in any way.

## Change Management

For the purpose of this guide, change management is limited to the considerations of change management, and does not specify the process itself. If you are interested in a detailed process-oriented view of infrastructure management, you should refer to IT Infrastructure Library (ITIL) and to the Microsoft Operations Framework (MOF).

Change management is particularly important for effective application integration. Any integration application relies on a number of other applications, each of which is susceptible to changes from its respective owner. Changes to these applications are likely to have a significant impact on the integration application itself. Because the sheer volume of changes required can be large, having effective change management processes and tools helps to reduce the chance of errors when applying changes. Change management can also help to reduce the amount of time required for changes to be applied.

An important goal of having a change management system and process is to allow controlled changes to occur in the shortest period of time. Controlled change is an important criterion in maintaining a stable system. Without controlled changes, a system modification can produce undesirable results.

There are a number of items to consider when you establish your change management procedures:

- **Release management**. Release management involves planning how the change will be released as well as determining rollback or roll forward plans. Rollback entails reversing the changes and ensuring that the system is restored to the exact same configuration it was in prior to the release. Roll forward is necessary when the changes are known in advance to be irreversible. In such cases, it is vital to have plans in place to mitigate the risk of the system not functioning correctly. Ultimately, due to the possibility of frequent changes that can occur in an integration application, providing as much automation as possible will help speed the implementation of changes and reduce the risk of human error.

- **Regression testing**. Regression-testing the new application ensures that it does not compromise existing functionality. When the regression testing methodology and steps are well-defined, automating this process can help during release management and can reduce human-related errors.

- **Backward compatibility**. Backward compatibility is especially relevant in the integration area. Backward compatibility allows the functionality of the integration application to be enhanced or modified without affecting existing systems that relied on the application.

## Directory

The Directory capability is essential in the context of integration, because it stores much of the information required by application integration.

Generally available directory systems are highly scalable and often reside across multiple physical servers. As a result, normally a delay occurs before changes to data are consistently presented across all physical servers. Hence, if the data stored in the directory changes often—a few times a minute, for example—the directory may never present a consistent view of that data across all physical servers. For this reason, directories normally provide fairly static information that changes a maximum of a few times a day. Application interaction with the directory is largely restricted to read-only interactions.

The directories that are used in an application integration environment include:

- The identity directory, which is primarily used for security as the repository for identities and related information.
- Subscription directory, which is primarily used in a publish/subscribe scenario.
- Application configuration, which is primarily used by the applications themselves and stores configuration information.
- Capabilities directory, which provides a list of capabilities offered.

The identity directory is the repository of all user and system identities. It may also contain other related information such as the user roles and profile information. Many organizations aim to have a unified identity directory, but struggle to do so, due to the number of preexisting applications and the custom developed security mechanisms they use. The problem is exacerbated due to the number of different environments the applications are using.

The subscription directory, as the name implies, keeps track of subscribers. This directory is typically used in publish/subscribe communication. A separate directory ensures that the subscriber base can be managed outside the application logic, which allows for either self-subscription or total management of subscribers, or for a combination of both.

The application configuration directory is most useful in providing a consistent application configuration across a number of systems. For example, if an integration system currently requires 10 different servers and relies on a local configuration file, the operator must ensure that all 10 are consistent. Providing an application configuration directory allows these settings to be provided in a single location. Although there are tools that can assist to maintain the files, using them introduces another level of complexity, and there may be limitations in how the tools can replicate the configuration files to the servers.

The capabilities directory provides a common place where capabilities can be listed and used. In the case of Web capabilities, Universal Discovery Description and Integration (UDDI) servers provide this functionality. Regardless of whether the capabilities directory is a UDDI server or a custom server, it is important to ensure that the information reflects the type of capabilities provided in a commonly understood format and protocol. Commonly understood, in this case, can mean organization-wide or even spanning across to partner organizations.

# Index

## A

ACID requirements, 45–46, 115
  implementing, with DTC, 77
  long-running transactions
    and, 49
  satisfying, when coordinating
    different data states/
    messaging systems, 47
  satisfying, when transaction is
    widely dispersed, 47
  software designed for, 46
  transaction compensation
    and, 48
  Transactional Delivery
    capability and, 115
Active Directory Service Interfaces
  (ADSI), 72
Active Directory, 72, 94
active event handling, 122
addressing, 111
aggregation, 108, 40
  complexity of, 40
  processing requirements for, 40
  system monitoring and, 63
Analysis Services, 71–72, 93
APIs, vs. direct data access, 13
application configuration, 126–127
application integration
  architectural issues, 14
  automated. *See* automated
    application integration
  benefits of, 3
  business process-level. *See*
    business process integration
  choosing appropriate type of, 5
  communications-level. *See*
    communications integration
  data-level. *See* data integration
  defined, 3
  efficiency of, 5

environments. *See* environments
fully automated, 5–6
governance processes,
  establishing, 15
implementing. *See* implementing
  application integration
integration hub environment,
  8–9
manual, 4–5
mapping business process
  requirements to, 23
Microsoft technologies for. *See*
  Microsoft technologies
open standards, basing on, 11.
  *See also* Web services
organizing, 14
people and, 5–6
point-to-point environment, 7–8
requirements for, 10
scalability of. *See* scalability
semi-automated. *See* semi-
  automated application
  integration
structuring, 7–10
technical issues, 14
application programming
  interfaces (APIs), vs. direct
  data access, 13
applications
  ACID requirements. *See* ACID
    requirements
  communication, 26–28
  composed. *See* composed
    applications
  directory-enabled, creating, 72
  enabling communication
    between, by rewriting with
    APIs vs. creating
    communications adaptors, 27

  enabling to convert incoming/
    outgoing data into
    intermediary format, 25
  enabling to understand data
    from other applications, lack
    of scalability of, 25
  failures, detecting, 65
  functionality for receiving and
    interpreting messages. *See*
    composed applications
  functionality, combining, 40
  internal resources, accessing
    with program calls, 12
  Microsoft. *See* Microsoft
    technologies
  reusing parts of, 40
architectural issues, 14
ASP.NET state management, 78
asynchronous communication
  benefits of, 29
  capabilities required for, 29
  vs. synchronous communication,
    28
atomic transactions. *See* ACID
  requirements
Atomicity, Consistency, Isolation,
  and Durability requirements.
  *See* ACID requirements
authentication, 56–57, 117
  in BizTalk Server, 91
  choosing appropriate type of, 56
  HTTP Basic, 56
  Kerberos, 56
  Microsoft technologies and, 91
  multifactorial, 56–57
  not integrated with operating
    system, 57
  password management, 57

# patterns & practices

proven practices for predictable results

## About Microsoft *patterns & practices*

Microsoft *patterns & practices* guides contain specific recommendations illustrating how to design, build, deploy, and operate architecturally sound solutions to challenging business and technical scenarios. They offer deep technical guidance based on real-world experience that goes far beyond white papers to help enterprise IT professionals, information workers, and developers quickly deliver sound solutions.

IT Professionals, information workers, and developers can choose from four types of *patterns & practices*:

- **Patterns**—Patterns are a consistent way of documenting solutions to commonly occurring problems. Patterns are available that address specific architecture, design, and implementation problems. Each pattern also has an associated GotDotNet Community.

- **Reference Architectures**—Reference Architectures are IT system-level architectures that address the business requirements, LifeCycle requirements, and technical constraints for commonly occurring scenarios. Reference Architectures focus on planning the architecture of IT systems.

- **Reference Building Blocks and IT Services**—References Building Blocks and IT Services are re-usable sub-system designs that address common technical challenges across a wide range of scenarios. Many include tested reference implementations to accelerate development. Reference Building Blocks and IT Services focus on the design and implementation of sub-systems.

- **Lifecycle Practices**—Lifecycle Practices provide guidance for tasks outside the scope of architecture and design such as deployment and operations in a production environment.

*Patterns & practices* guides are reviewed and approved by Microsoft engineering teams, consultants, Product Support Services, and by partners and customers. *Patterns & practices* guides are:

- **Proven**—They are based on field experience.
- **Authoritative**—They offer the best advice available.
- **Accurate**—They are technically validated and tested.
- **Actionable**—They provide the steps to success.
- **Relevant**—They address real-world problems based on customer scenarios.

To learn more about *patterns & practices* visit: **http://msdn.microsoft.com/practices**
To purchase *patterns & practices* guides visit: **http://shop.microsoft.com/practices**

*Patterns & practices* guides are designed to help IT professionals, information workers, and developers:

## Reduce project cost

- Exploit the Microsoft engineering efforts to save time and money on your projects.
- Follow the Microsoft recommendations to lower your project risk and achieve predictable outcomes.

## Increase confidence in solutions

- Build your solutions on proven Microsoft recommendations so you can have total confidence in your results.
- Rely on thoroughly tested and supported guidance, but production quality recommendations and code, not just samples.

## Deliver strategic IT advantage

- Solve your problems today and take advantage of future Microsoft technologies with practical advice.

To learn more about *patterns & practices* visit: **http://msdn.microsoft.com/practices**
To purchase *patterns & practices* guides visit: **http://shop.microsoft.com/practices**

# patterns & practices: Current Titles

October 2003

| Title | Link to Online Version | Book |
|---|---|---|
| **Patterns** | | |
| Enterprise Solution Patterns using Microsoft .NET | *http://msdn.microsoft.com/practices/type/Patterns /Enterprise/default.asp* | ▣ |
| Microsoft Data Patterns | *http://msdn.microsoft.com/practices/type/Patterns /Data/default.asp* | |
| **Reference Architectures** | | |
| Application Architecture for .NET: Designing Applications and Services | *http://msdn.microsoft.com/library/default.asp?url= /library/en-us/dnbda/html/distapp.asp* | ▣ |
| Enterprise Notification Reference Architecture for Exchange 2000 Server | *http://msdn.microsoft.com/library/default.asp?url= /library/en-us/dnentdevgen/html/enraelp.asp* | |
| Improving Web Application Security: Threats and Countermeasures | *http://msdn.microsoft.com/library/default.asp?url= /library/en-us/dnnetsec/html/ThreatCounter.asp* | ▣ |
| Microsoft Accelerator for Six Sigma | *http://www.microsoft.com/technet/treeview /default.asp?url=/technet/itsolutions/mso/sixsigma /default.asp* | |
| Microsoft Active Directory Branch Office Guide: Volume 1: Planning | *http://www.microsoft.com/technet/treeview /default.asp?url=/technet/prodtechnol/ad /windows2000/deploy/adguide/default.asp* | ▣ |
| Microsoft Active Directory Branch Office Series Volume 2: Deployment and Operations | *http://www.microsoft.com/technet/treeview /default.asp?url=/technet/prodtechnol/ad /windows2000/deploy/adguide/default.asp* | ▣ |
| Microsoft Content Integration Pack for Content Management Server 2001 and SharePoint Portal Server 2001 | *http://msdn.microsoft.com/library/default.asp?url= /library/en-us/dncip/html/cip.asp* | |
| Microsoft Exchange 2000 Server Hosting Series Volume 1: Planning | Online Version not available | ▣ |
| Microsoft Exchange 2000 Server Hosting Series Volume 2: Deployment | Online Version not available | ▣ |

| Title | Link to Online Version | Book |
|-------|------------------------|------|
| Microsoft Exchange 2000 Server Upgrade Series Volume 1: Planning | *http://www.microsoft.com/technet/treeview /default.asp?url=/technet/itsolutions/guide /default.asp* | |
| Microsoft Exchange 2000 Server Upgrade Series Volume 2: Deployment | http://www.microsoft.com/technet/treeview /default.asp?url=/technet/itsolutions/guide /default.asp | |
| Microsoft Solution for Intranets | *http://www.microsoft.com/technet/treeview /default.asp?url=/technet/itsolutions/mso /msi/Default.asp* | |
| Microsoft Solution for Securing Wireless LANs | *http://www.microsoft.com/downloads /details.aspx?FamilyId=CDB639B3-010B-47E7-B23 4-A27CDA291DAD&displaylang=en* | |
| Microsoft Systems Architecture— Enterprise Data Center | *http://www.microsoft.com/technet/treeview /default.asp?url=/technet/itsolutions/edc /Default.asp* | |
| Microsoft Systems Architecture— Internet Data Center | *http://www.microsoft.com/technet/treeview/ default.asp?url=/technet/itsolutions/idc/default.asp* | |
| The Enterprise Project Management Solution | *http://www.microsoft.com/technet/treeview /default.asp?url=/technet/itsolutions/mso/epm /default.asp* | |
| UNIX Application Migration Guide | *http://msdn.microsoft.com/library/default.asp?url= /library/en-us/dnucmg/html/ucmglp.asp* | |
| **Reference Building Blocks and IT Services** | | |
| .NET Data Access Architecture Guide | *http://msdn.microsoft.com/library/default.asp?url= /library/en-us/dnbda/html/daag.asp* | |
| Application Updater Application Block | *http://msdn.microsoft.com/library/default.asp?url= /library/en-us/dnbda/html/updater.asp* | |
| Asynchronous Invocation Application Block | *http://msdn.microsoft.com/library/default.asp?url= /library/en-us/dnpag/html/paiblock.asp* | |
| Authentication in ASP.NET: .NET Security Guidance | *http://msdn.microsoft.com/library/default.asp?url= /library/en-us/dnbda/html/authaspdotnet.asp* | |
| Building Interoperable Web Services: WS-I Basic Profile 1.0 | *http://msdn.microsoft.com/library/default.asp?url= /library/en-us/dnsvcinter/html/wsi-bp_msdn_ landingpage.asp* | |
| Building Secure ASP.NET Applications: Authentication, Authorization, and Secure Communication | *http://msdn.microsoft.com/library/default.asp?url= /library/en-us/dnnetsec/html/secnetlpMSDN.asp* | |

| Title | Link to Online Version | Book |
|-------|------------------------|------|
| Caching Application Block | *http://msdn.microsoft.com/library/default.asp?url= /library/en-us/dnpag/html/Cachingblock.asp* | |
| Caching Architecture Guide for .Net Framework Applications | *http://msdn.microsoft.com/library/default.asp?url= /library/en-us/dnbda/html/CachingArch.asp?frame= true* | |
| Configuration Management Application Block | *http://msdn.microsoft.com/library/default.asp?url= /library/en-us/dnbda/html/cmab.asp* | |
| Data Access Application Block for .NET | *http://msdn.microsoft.com/library/default.asp?url= /library/en-us/dnbda/html/daab-rm.asp* | |
| Designing Application-Managed Authorization | *http://msdn.microsoft.com/library/?url=/library /en-us/dnbda/html/damaz.asp* | |
| Designing Data Tier Components and Passing Data Through Tiers | *http://msdn.microsoft.com/library/default.asp?url= /library/en-us/dnbda/html/BOAGag.asp* | |
| Exception Management Application Block for .NET | *http://msdn.microsoft.com/library/default.asp?url= /library/en-us/dnbda/html/emab-rm.asp* | |
| Exception Management Architecture Guide | *http://msdn.microsoft.com/library/default.asp?url= /library/en-us/dnbda/html/exceptdotnet.asp* | |
| Microsoft .NET/COM Migration and Interoperability | *http://msdn.microsoft.com/library/default.asp?url= /library/en-us/dnbda/html/cominterop.asp* | |
| Microsoft Windows Server 2003 Security Guide | *http://www.microsoft.com/downloads/ details.aspx?FamilyId=8A2643C1-0685-4D89-B655- 521EA6C7B4DB&displaylang=en* | |
| Monitoring in .NET Distributed Application Design | *http://msdn.microsoft.com/library/default.asp?url= /library/en-us/dnbda/html/monitordotnet.asp* | |
| New Application Installation using Systems Management Server | *http://www.microsoft.com/business/reducecosts /efficiency/manageability/application.mspx* | |
| Patch Management using Microsoft Systems Management Server - Operations Guide | *http://www.microsoft.com/technet/treeview/ default.asp?url=/technet/itsolutions/msm/swdist/ pmsms/pmsmsog.asp* | |
| Patch Management Using Microsoft Software Update Services - Operations Guide | *http://www.microsoft.com/technet/treeview/ default.asp?url=/technet/itsolutions/msm/swdist/ pmsus/pmsusog.asp* | |
| Service Aggregation Application Block | *http://msdn.microsoft.com/library/default.asp?url= /library/en-us/dnpag/html/serviceagg.asp* | |
| Service Monitoring and Control using Microsoft Operations Manager | *http://www.microsoft.com/business/reducecosts /efficiency/manageability/monitoring.mspx* | |

| Title | Link to Online Version | Book |
|---|---|---|
| User Interface Process Application Block | *http://msdn.microsoft.com/library/default.asp?url= /library/en-us/dnbda/html/uip.asp* | |
| Web Service Façade for Legacy Applications | *http://msdn.microsoft.com/library/default.asp?url= /library/en-us/dnpag/html/wsfacadelegacyapp.asp* | |
| **Lifecycle Practices** | | |
| Backup and Restore for Internet Data Center | *http://www.microsoft.com/technet/treeview/default.asp ?url=/technet/ittasks/maintain/backuprest/Default.asp* | |
| Deploying .NET Applications: Lifecycle Guide | *http://msdn.microsoft.com/library/default.asp?url= /library/en-us/dnbda/html/DALGRoadmap.asp* | |
| Microsoft Exchange 2000 Server Operations Guide | *http://www.microsoft.com/technet/treeview/default. asp?url=/technet/prodtechnol/exchange/exchange 2000/maintain/operate/opsguide/default.asp* |  |
| Microsoft SQL Server 2000 High Availability Series: Volume 1: Planning | *http://www.microsoft.com/technet/treeview /default.asp?url=/technet/prodtechnol/sql/deploy /confeat/sqlha/SQLHALP.asp* |  |
| Microsoft SQL Server 2000 High Availability Series: Volume 2: Deployment | *http://www.microsoft.com/technet/treeview /default.asp?url=/technet/prodtechnol/sql/deploy /confeat/sqlha/SQLHALP.asp* |  |
| Microsoft SQL Server 2000 Operations Guide | *http://www.microsoft.com/technet/treeview /default.asp?url=/technet/prodtechnol/sql/maintain /operate/opsguide/default.asp* | |
| Operating .NET-Based Applications | *http://www.microsoft.com/technet/treeview /default.asp?url=/technet/itsolutions/net/maintain /opnetapp/default.asp* |  |
| Production Debugging for .NET-Connected Applications | *http://msdn.microsoft.com/library/default.asp?url= /library/en-us/dnbda/html/DBGrm.asp* | |
| Security Operations for Microsoft Windows 2000 Server | *http://www.microsoft.com/technet/treeview /default.asp?url=/technet/security/prodtech /win2000/secwin2k/default.asp* |  |
| Security Operations Guide for Exchange 2000 Server | *http://www.microsoft.com/technet/treeview /default.asp?url=/technet/security/prodtech /mailexch/opsguide/default.asp* |  |
| Team Development with Visual Studio .NET and Visual SourceSafe | *http://msdn.microsoft.com/library/default.asp?url= /library/en-us/dnbda/html/tdlg_rm.asp* | |

 This title is available as a Book